D1460460

JOURNEYS

Reader's Notebook

Volume 2

Grade 3

HOUGHTON MIFFLIN HARCOURT
School Publishers

Copyright © by Houghton Mifflin Harcourt Publishing Company

All rights reserved. No part of this work may be reproduced or transmitted in any form or by any means, electronic or mechanical, including photocopying or recording, or by any information storage or retrieval system, without the prior written permission of the copyright owner unless such copying is expressly permitted by federal copyright law.

Permission is hereby granted to individuals using the corresponding student's textbook or kit as the major vehicle for regular classroom instruction to photocopy entire pages from this publication in classroom quantities for instructional use and not for resale. Requests for information on other matters regarding duplication of this work should be addressed to Houghton Mifflin Harcourt Publishing Company, Attn: Contracts, Copyrights, and Licensing, 9400 Southpark Center Loop, Orlando, Florida 32819.

Printed in the U.S.A.

ISBN 978-0-547-86066-4

35 0928 21

4500821583 B C D E F G

If you have received these materials as examination copies free of charge, Houghton Mifflin Harcourt Publishing Company retains title to the materials and they may not be resold. Resale of examination copies is strictly prohibited.

Possession of this publication in print format does not entitle users to convert this publication, or any portion of it, into electronic format.

Contents

Unit 4

Lesson 16:	Judy Moody Saves the World!	1
Lesson 17:	The Albertosaurus Mystery: Philip Currie's Hunt in the Badlands	15
Lesson 18:	A Tree Is Growing	29
Lesson 19:	Two Bear Cubs	43
Lesson 20:	Life on the Ice	57

Unit 5

Lesson 21:	Sarah, Plain and Tall	89
Lesson 22:	The Journey: Stories of Migration	103
Lesson 23:	The Journey of Oliver K. Woodman	117
Lesson 24:	Dog-of-the-Sea-Waves	131
Lesson 25:	Mountains: Surviving on Mt. Everest	145

Unit 6

Lesson 26:	The Foot Race Across America	159
Lesson 27:	The Power of Magnets	171
Lesson 28:	Becoming Anything He Wants to Be	183
Lesson 29:	A New Team of Heroes	195
Lesson 30:	Saving Buster	207

© Houghton Mifflin Harcourt Publishing Company. All rights reserved.

Name ______________________ Date ______________

Judy Moody Saves the World!
Phonics:
Words with *air, ear, are*

Words with *air*, *ear*, *are*

Write a word from the box to complete each sentence. Then read the complete sentence.

airfare	hear	wear
airline	pear	year
dairy	share	
prepare	tear	

1. The ______________ has ten airplanes.
2. Gently ______________ the paper into two pieces.
3. The teacher will ______________ the lesson for the day.
4. Did you ______________ the bell ring?
5. You must pay the ______________ before you can ride on the plane.
6. Milk and cheese are in the ______________ food group.
7. You and I were born in the same ______________.
8. It's cold outside, so you'll need to ______________ your coat.
9. This is a juicy ______________!
10. It's kind to ______________ your toys.

© Houghton Mifflin Harcourt Publishing Company. All rights reserved.

Name ____________________ Date __________

Adjectives That Tell What Kind

Adjectives are words that describe, or tell about, nouns. Some adjectives tell what kind.

We went for a long walk. (What kind of walk?)

An adjective usually comes before the noun it describes.

Thinking Question
Which word tells what kind?

Write the adjective that tells about the underlined noun.

1. Our class started a recycling project. ______________
2. Mr. Thomas put several big bins in the room. ______________
3. The blue bin was for paper. ______________
4. Jason added a stack of old newspapers. ______________
5. Lee Ann brought wrapping paper. ______________
6. Melissa used the colorful paper for a collage. ______________
7. We added our cereal boxes to the bin. ______________
8. Our small class collected a lot of paper. ______________
9. We took the bins to a green truck. ______________
10. The workers wore thick gloves. ______________

© Houghton Mifflin Harcourt Publishing Company. All rights reserved.

Name ______________________ Date ____________

Adjectives That Tell How Many

An **adjective** is a word that describes, or tells about, a noun. Some adjectives tell how many. An adjective that tells how many comes before the noun it describes.

She saw three birds in a nest. (How many birds?)

Thinking Question
Which word tells how many?

Write the adjective that tells about the underlined noun.

1. There are two paths along the river. ______________
2. My dad hikes to the river with four friends. ______________
3. They bring five bags to collect trash. ______________
4. My dad picks up many cans. ______________
5. Soon two bags are filled with trash. ______________
6. Then they see several cans in the shallow river. ______________
7. Three men have boots and wade into the water. ______________
8. They use a net and pull seventeen cans out of the river. ______________
9. A few more pieces of trash are under the bench. ______________
10. Their walk home is about one mile. ______________

© Houghton Mifflin Harcourt Publishing Company. All rights reserved.

Name ______________________ Date ____________

Spelling Word Sort

Write each Basic Word under the correct heading.

Vowel + /r/ Sound in *air* spelled *air*	**Vowel + /r/ Sound in *fear* spelled *ear***
____________	____________
____________	____________
____________	____________
____________	____________
____________	____________
Vowel + /r/ Sound in *air* spelled *ear*	**Vowel + /r/ Sound in *air* spelled *are***
____________	____________
____________	____________
____________	____________
____________	____________

Review **Add one Review Word to your Word Sort.**

Which Review Word cannot be added to the Word Sort?

____

Challenge: **Add the Challenge Words to your Word Sort.**

Spelling Words

Basic

1. air
2. wear
3. chair
4. stairs
5. bare
6. bear
7. hair
8. care
9. pear
10. pair
11. share
12. near
13. ear
14. beard

Review

buy
year

Challenge

earring
compare

© Houghton Mifflin Harcourt Publishing Company. All rights reserved.

Name ______________________ Date ____________

Focus Trait: Ideas

Introducing the Topic and Opinion

A persuasive letter tries to make someone believe something or take an action. Good writers state their opinion clearly and convince readers it is correct by giving specific reasons. For example, Monique does not like the school lunch menu because it includes too much junk food. She wants to convince the school board to change the menu so it includes more healthful foods, like fruits and vegetables. She might offer reasons, such as healthful foods help kids think better and have stronger bodies.

Read each writer's opinion and think about the writer's goal. Then read the reasons that could support the opinion. Underline the strongest, most convincing reasons.

1. We should help rescued dogs and cats. I want to convince people to adopt rescued animals.

REASONS

A. Pets are good.

B. Adopting a rescued pet saves a life.

C. Rescued pets have a lot of love to give owners.

D. Some rescued pets are injured or sick.

2. We should clean up our local park. I want to convince my classmates to volunteer to help clean up the park.

REASONS

A. Kids are getting hurt on broken glass and metal litter.

B. A lot of people use the park.

C. We can be proud of the place where we play.

D. Litter makes the park look bad.

© Houghton Mifflin Harcourt Publishing Company. All rights reserved.

Name ______________________ Date ____________

Cumulative Review

Judy Moody Saves the World!
Phonics:
Cumulative Review

Write a word from the box to complete each sentence in the story. Then read the story.

careful	energy	wear
center	shirt	worry
dirty	turned	
disappeared	stairs	

"I want to ______ (1) my new clothes," said Julia. She went up the ______ (2) to her room and put them on.

Julia went back downstairs. She ______ (3) the doorknob to go outside.

"Julia," said Mom, "don't get your new clothes ______ (4)."

"Don't ______ (5), Mom. I'll be ______ (6)!"

Julia ______ (7) into the backyard. She used a lot of ______ (8) playing outside. As she came back in, she saw a big spot in the ______ (9) of her new ______ (10). "Oh, no!" she gasped. "I should have listened to Mom!"

© Houghton Mifflin Harcourt Publishing Company. All rights reserved.

Reader's Guide

Judy Moody Saves the World!

Judy Moody's Class Presentation

"Judy Moody will come up to the front of the class and talk about what she has learned about the environment," said Mr. Todd.

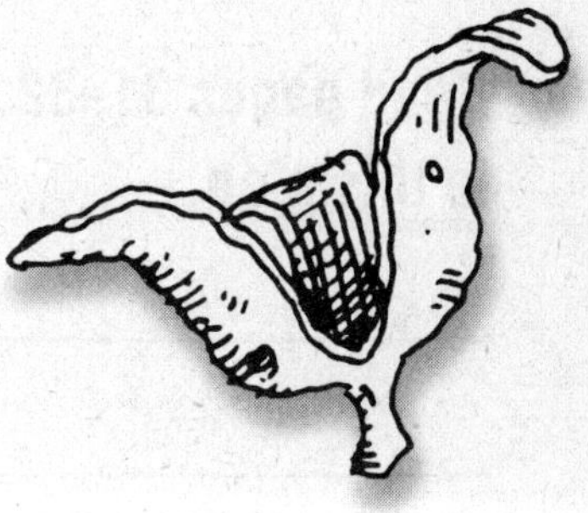

Read pages 18–20. Use the information on these pages to help Judy tell the class how she got the idea to save the world.

____

____

____

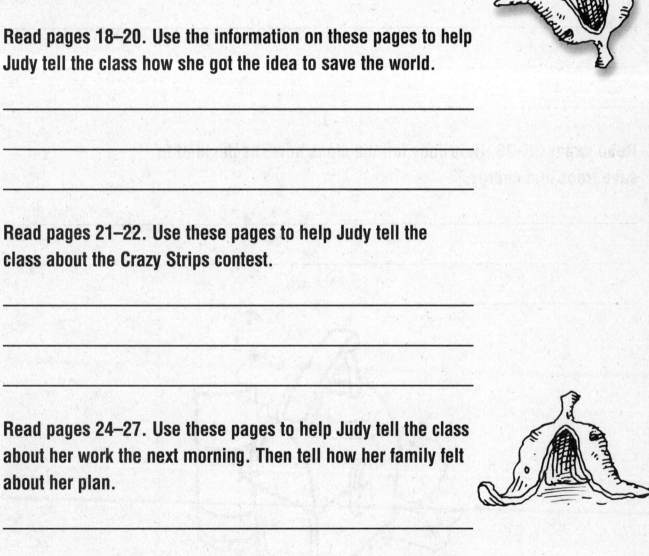

Read pages 21–22. Use these pages to help Judy tell the class about the Crazy Strips contest.

____

____

____

Read pages 24–27. Use these pages to help Judy tell the class about her work the next morning. Then tell how her family felt about her plan.

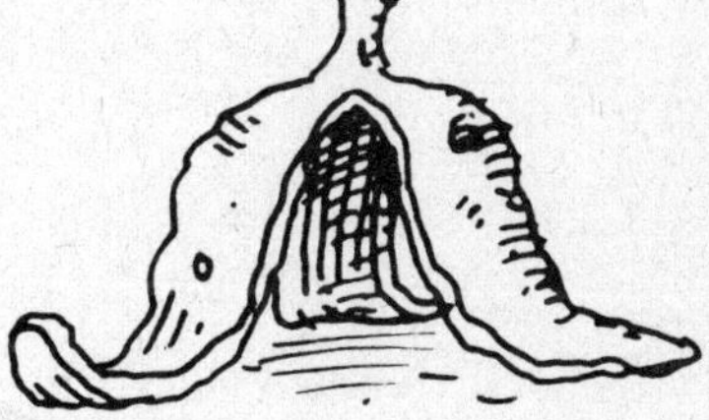

____

____

____

© Houghton Mifflin Harcourt Publishing Company. All rights reserved.

Name ______________________________ Date ________

Read pages 28–29. Use these pages to help Judy tell about her next plan.

____

____

____

Read pages 31–32. Help Judy tell how her family responded to this plan.

____

____

____

Read pages 35–36. Help Judy tell the class how she decided to save trees and energy.

____

____

____

© Houghton Mifflin Harcourt Publishing Company. All rights reserved.

Name ____________________ Date __________

This, That and Articles

- The adjectives *this* and *that* tell "which one."
- The words *a*, *an*, and *the* are adjectives called **articles.**
- Use *a* before nouns that begin with a consonant sound. Use *an* before nouns that begin with a vowel sound.

Underline the adjective that tells *which one*. Write the noun the adjective describes.

1. My friends and I helped clean this park. ____________
2. We put the trash we collected in that can. ____________
3. This playground could use a good cleaning. ____________

Choose the article in parentheses to go with the underlined word. Write the article.

4. I have (a, an) <u>can</u> to recycle. ____________
5. You should recycle (the, an) <u>paper</u>. ____________
6. There is (a, an) <u>empty</u> bin. ____________
7. (The, An) <u>bin</u> is not full yet. ____________

© Houghton Mifflin Harcourt Publishing Company. All rights reserved.

Name ______________________ Date ______________

Word Towers

Read each clue. Write the Basic Word that matches each clue.

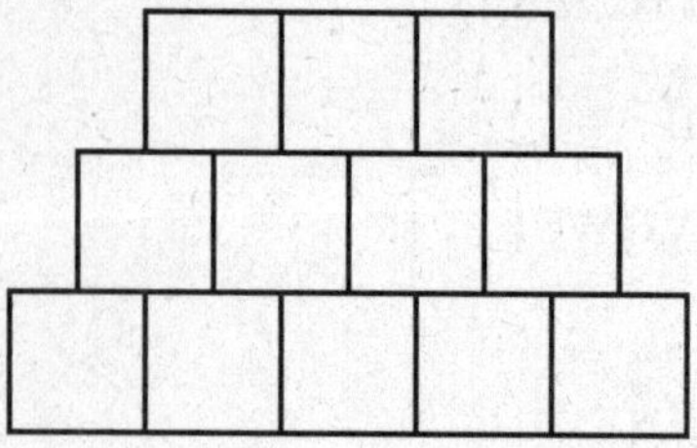

Clues

1. A body part you use to hear
2. Two of something
3. Hair on a man's chin

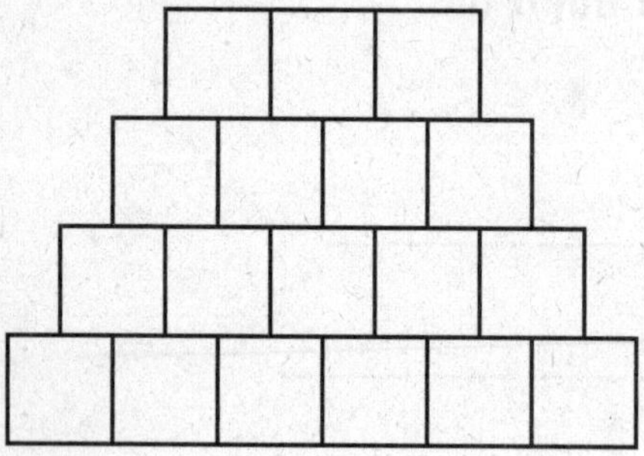

4. Fills the open space around you
5. A large, strong animal
6. Split something with a friend
7. Steps

Challenge Use Basic, Review, and Challenge Words to complete the Word Tower.

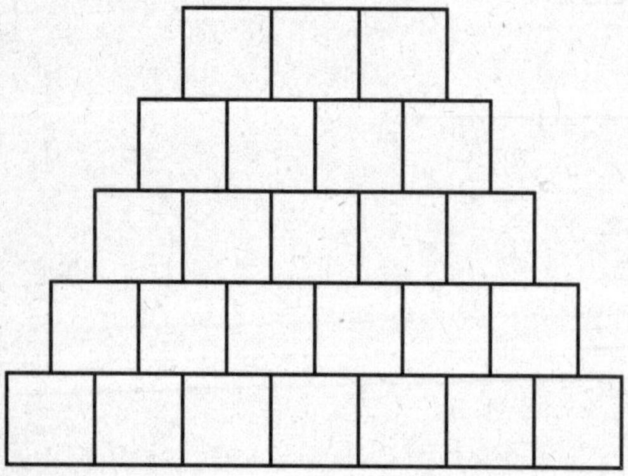

Clues

8. Pay money for something
9. Feel love and concern for someone
10. Furniture you can sit on
11. Steps
12. Tell how two things are alike

Spelling Words

Basic

1. air
2. wear
3. chair
4. stairs
5. bare
6. bear
7. hair
8. care
9. pear
10. pair
11. share
12. near
13. ear
14. beard

Review

buy
year

Challenge

earring
compare

© Houghton Mifflin Harcourt Publishing Company. All rights reserved.

Name ______________________ Date ____________

Judy Moody Saves the World!
Vocabulary Strategies:
Context Clues

Context Clues

Write the meaning of the underlined word as it is used in each sentence. Circle the words that help you know the meaning of the underlined word.

1. One weekend each fall, our family goes on a yearly campout.

____

2. When it gets dark, we gather kindling to start a campfire.

____

3. Last year, our tent was leaky. Rain dripped in while we were sleeping.

____

4. Our new tent is made from recycled bottles.

____

5. This year, we forgot to put our garbage in the trash can with a lid.

____

6. A raccoon gobbled up the food we threw away.

____

7. My brother and I quarreled with loud voices over who was supposed to put the lid on the trash can.

____

8. Pop got us to stop fighting when he suggested that we all go fishing.

____

9. We got the necessary gear to catch fish and headed to the pond.

____

10. We were sad to see the pollution in the pond.

____

© Houghton Mifflin Harcourt Publishing Company. All rights reserved.

Name ______________________ Date ____________

More Plural Nouns

- Form the **plural of a noun** that ends with a consonant and *y* by changing the *y* to *i* and adding *-es*.
- Identify nouns that change their spelling to form their plurals.

The families enjoyed watching the geese.

Write the plural form of each singular noun in parentheses.

1. two beautiful (butterfly) ______________

2. six new (hobby) ______________

3. two intelligent (woman) ______________

4. many falling (leaf) ______________

5. a crowd of (child) ______________

Write *singular* or *plural* for each underlined noun.

6. A man gathered bottles. ______________

7. The geese flew over the recycling area. ______________

8. Many families recycle their own garbage. ______________

9. One city saves money by reusing paper. ______________

10. Mice will eat garbage if it isn't cleaned up. ______________

© Houghton Mifflin Harcourt Publishing Company. All rights reserved.

Name ______________________ Date ______________

Judy Moody Saves the World!
Spelling:
Vowel + /r/ Sounds in *air* and *fear*

Proofreading for Spelling

Read the following journal entry. Find and circle the misspelled words.

May 8

Today I went camping in a park nere my home. Before I left, I took cair as I decided what to where. I put on a jacket because the aer was crisp. I put a cap over my haire. I wore a pare of hiking boots, too.

I got to the campsite and set up my tent. I sat in my camp chare and started to eat a juicy paire. All of a sudden I saw a big, brown bair. He was looking at my food, but I did not want to shear. I ended my camping trip right then and there!

Write the misspelled words correctly on the lines below.

1. ______________ 6. ______________
2. ______________ 7. ______________
3. ______________ 8. ______________
4. ______________ 9. ______________
5. ______________ 10. ______________

Spelling Words

Basic
1. air
2. wear
3. chair
4. stairs
5. bare
6. bear
7. hair
8. care
9. pear
10. pair
11. share
12. near
13. ear
14. beard

Review
buy
year

Challenge
earring
compare

© Houghton Mifflin Harcourt Publishing Company. All rights reserved.

Name ______________________ Date ____________

Connect to Writing

Short Sentences	Longer, Smoother Sentence
Our class watched a video about recycling. The video about recycling was interesting.	Our class watched an interesting video about recycling.
There was a talking can in the video. The talking can was green.	There was a green talking can in the video.

Combine two short sentences by moving an adjective to make one longer sentence. Write the new sentence on the line.

1. The video was about a recycling center. The recycling center was big.

   ____

2. Many people work in the recycling center. It is noisy in the recycling center.

   ____

3. One worker wore a hat. The hat was huge.

   ____

4. The wind blew paper into the air. The paper was yellow.

   ____

5. The workers take a bus home. The bus is new.

   ____

© Houghton Mifflin Harcourt Publishing Company. All rights reserved.

Name ____________________ Date __________

Words with /j/ and /s/

Read each sentence. Choose the missing word from the box. Write the word. Then reread the complete sentence.

season	decide	squirt
jelly	scale	jumping
force	edge	engine

1. Which ______________ of the year is your favorite?
2. Close the door with ______________.
3. I would love to drive a fire ______________!
4. Place the apples on the ______________.
5. Felice likes to put ______________ on her toast.
6. The ______________ on these scissors is too dull to cut cardboard.
7. "Did you ______________ who is the winner?" the girl asked.
8. If you ______________ me with water, I'll have to change my clothes.
9. We saw grasshoppers ______________ into the bushes.

© Houghton Mifflin Harcourt Publishing Company. All rights reserved.

Name ____________________ Date ____________

Adding *-er*, *-ier*, or *More*

- Add *-er* to most **adjectives** that have one syllable.
- For adjectives that have two syllables and end in *-y*, such as *happy*, replace the *y* with *i* and then add *-er*.
- Add *more* before adjectives that have two or more syllables.

  The pottery is larger than the arrowheads.
  The arrowheads were shinier than the pottery.
  The Native American exhibit is more modern than the dinosaur exhibit.

Thinking Questions
Does the adjective have more than one syllable? Does it end in -y?

Choose the correct form of the adjective in parentheses. Write it on the line.

1. The (younger, more young) of the two students found an arrowhead made of stone. ____________
2. The arrowhead was in a location (deeper, more deep) than the clay pot. ____________
3. One of the bones was (tinier, more tiny) than the arrowhead. ____________
4. It was (difficulter, more difficult) to unearth the arrowheads than the bones. ____________
5. The circle of stones was (interestinger, more interesting) than the bones they found. ____________

© Houghton Mifflin Harcourt Publishing Company. All rights reserved.

Name ____________________ Date __________

One-Syllable Adjectives That Compare

- Add *-er* to most **adjectives** that have one syllable.
- For adjectives with one syllable that end in a single vowel followed by a consonant, double the last consonant and then add *-er*.

Are the Badlands hotter than a desert?

Thinking Question
Does the adjective have only one syllable and end in a single vowel followed by a consonant?

Write the correct form of the adjective that compares two nouns.

1. fresh ____________________
2. green ____________________
3. fat ____________________
4. sad ____________________
5. hard ____________________
6. cool ____________________
7. thin ____________________
8. tight ____________________
9. soft ____________________
10. ripe ____________________

© Houghton Mifflin Harcourt Publishing Company. All rights reserved.

Name ______________________ Date ____________

Spelling Words with /j/ and /s/

The Albertosaurus Mystery
Spelling:
Words with /j/ and /s/

Spelling Words

Basic
1. age
2. space
3. change
4. jawbone
5. jacket
6. giant
7. pencil
8. circle
9. once
10. large
11. dance
12. jeans
13. bounce
14. huge

Review
nice
place

Challenge
excited
gigantic

1. Write the Basic Words that use the letter *j* to spell the sound /j/.

   ____________, ____________,
   ____

2. Write the Basic Words that use the letter *g* to spell the sound /j/.

   ____________, ____________,
   ____________, ____________,
   ____

3. Write the Basic Word that uses the letter *s* to spell the sound /s/.

   ____

4. Write the Basic Words that use the letter *c* to spell the sound /s/.

   ____________, ____________,
   ____________, ____________,
   ____________, ____________

Challenge

1. **gigantic** Circle the letter in *gigantic* that makes one of this week's spelling sounds.
2. **excited** Circle the letter in *excited* that makes one of this week's spelling sounds.

© Houghton Mifflin Harcourt Publishing Company. All rights reserved.

Name ______________________ Date ____________

Focus Trait: Voice

Convincing Voice

Good writers of opinion paragraphs use a convincing voice. If you provide interesting details, your opinion will be stronger and more convincing. Compare these sentences:

Weak Voice: I think computers are a waste of time.

Convincing Voice: Computers can be a big help doing some tasks, but it's important to do more than just sit in front of a monitor all day. How about getting outside and playing with friends?

Read each sentence. Revise sentences with weak voice to be more convincing.

1. **Weak Voice:** Our cafeteria food is not very good.
   Convincing Voice: ______________________________

2. **Weak Voice:** I think school sports are great.
   Convincing Voice: ______________________________

3. **Weak Voice:** I think homework should be more fun.
   Convincing Voice: ______________________________

© Houghton Mifflin Harcourt Publishing Company. All rights reserved.

Name ______________________ Date ____________

Words with the VCCCV Pattern

Write a word from the box to complete each sentence. Then read the complete sentence.

explore	partner	improve
instant	complaining	laundry
complicated	dolphin	athlete

1. I know that if I practice I will ______________.

2. We made ______________ oatmeal since we had no time to cook breakfast.

3. Cara is a great ______________ who swims and plays soccer.

4. When we paired up, I chose Gloria as my ______________.

5. Tran is always ______________ that it is too cold.

6. This puzzle is too ______________ for young children.

7. When we were at the beach, we saw a ______________ in the sea.

8. Mom is teaching me to do my own ______________.

9. I would like to travel and ______________ the world.

© Houghton Mifflin Harcourt Publishing Company. All rights reserved.

Name ____________________ Date ______

Reader's Guide

The Albertosaurus Mystery: Philip Currie's Hunt in the Badlands

Clues in the Attic

You are exploring an old attic and you find a large wooden chest. You read the name *Barnum Brown* scrolled across the back. The chest must belong to Barnum Brown! As you uncover each object inside the chest, help tell the story of Barnum Brown's discoveries.

First, you find a photograph of an old plow.

Read page 64. Use what you learn on this page and write why Barnum Brown kept this photo.

____

____

____

You continue digging through the chest and find a photograph of T. rex bones.

Read page 65. Use information from this page to decide why this photograph was important to Barnum Brown.

____

____

____

© Houghton Mifflin Harcourt Publishing Company. All rights reserved.

Name ______________________________ Date ________

Inside the wooden chest, you also find an old journal wrapped in cloth. You open to a page and begin reading Philip Currie's journal entries.

Read pages 69–70. What did Philip Curie write in his journal about his findings in the museum basement? What did he do as a result? Write as if you are Philip Curie.

____

____

____

Read pages 71–72. Use this information to write in Philip Currie's journal about his main question.

____

____

____

Read pages 73–75. Use this information to write in Currie's journal about Rodolfo Coria and what the two scientists concluded.

____

____

____

© Houghton Mifflin Harcourt Publishing Company. All rights reserved.

Name ______________________ Date __________

Comparing More Than Two Nouns

- Add *-est* to most **adjectives** that have one syllable.
- For adjectives with two or more syllables, add the word *most* before the adjective.
- For adjectives with two syllables that end in *-y*, such as *happy*, replace the *y* with an *i* and then add *-est*.
- For adjectives that have one syllable and end in a single vowel followed by a consonant, first double the last consonant and then add *-est*.

Which of the world's oceans is the deepest?

She chose the most expensive book.

Of the three jokes, Ben's is the funniest.

Thinking Questions
Does the adjective compare more than two nouns? Does it have more than one syllable? Does it end in -y?

Write the correct form of the adjective that compares more than two nouns.

1. happy ______________
2. wonderful ______________
3. fast ______________
4. thin ______________
5. sleepy ______________
6. dangerous ______________

© Houghton Mifflin Harcourt Publishing Company. All rights reserved.

Name ______________________ Date __________

Spelling Words with /j/ and /s/

1. Four of the words on the list are synonyms for *big*. Write them on the lines. You may write Basic Words and Challenge Words.

______________, ______________,

______________, ______________

2. Write three sentences about a dinosaur. Use four of the spelling words. Don't use any synonyms for *big*!

____

____

____

____

____

____

Spelling Words

Basic

1. age
2. space
3. change
4. jawbone
5. jacket
6. giant
7. pencil
8. circle
9. once
10. large
11. dance
12. jeans
13. bounce
14. huge

Review

nice
place

Challenge

excited
gigantic

© Houghton Mifflin Harcourt Publishing Company. All rights reserved.

Name ______________________ Date ____________

The Albertosaurus Mystery
Vocabulary Strategies: Suffix *-ly*

Suffix *-ly*

Circle the word in each sentence that has the suffix *-ly*. On the line, write the meaning of the word.

1. The angry dog growled fiercely.

____

2. The truck driver honked the horn loudly when the light turned green.

____

3. Maria won the race easily because she is the fastest runner in our class.

____

4. We watched hopefully as Sean tried to score the winning goal.

____

5. When he saw his birthday present, Jason laughed happily.

____

6. The students read quietly in the library until the bell rang.

____

7. Mom told Sara that she sang beautifully in the school play.

____

8. We walked carefully across the shaky bridge.

____

© Houghton Mifflin Harcourt Publishing Company. All rights reserved.

Writing Proper Nouns

- A **proper noun** names a particular person, pet, place, holiday, person's title, or book title.
- Always begin a proper noun with a capital letter.

  Aunt Liz took me to the Museum of Natural History.

Identify the proper nouns in each sentence. Then write each sentence correctly.

1. My favorite holiday is hanukkah and it is in december.

____

2. That is one of mrs. hubbard's favorite movies.

____

Use proofreading marks to write each proper noun in this letter correctly.

Dear grandma,

Last week our class at beacon school learned about cats. We looked at a book called all kinds of cats. My friend tracy brought her cat to class. Her cat's name is fuzzy. Her cat was a valentine's day present.

Love,
Amy

© Houghton Mifflin Harcourt Publishing Company. All rights reserved.

Name ____________________ Date ____________

Proofreading for Spelling

Find the misspelled words and circle them.

A long, long time ago, a jiant ship flew through outer spase. It was the shape of a pensil, but it was gijantic. It flew in a sircle around the Earth. It flew around the Earth onse, then twice, then three times. In fact, it flew around the Earth a hundred times! What was it doing? What was it looking for? No one knows. Maybe the people on the ship wanted to chanje planets. Maybe they liked to bounse from world to world and never stop. Maybe their world was not larje enough for them. I have a different answer, though. I think they were looking for a place to buy geans. They just came here thousands of years too soon.

Spelling Words

1. age
2. space
3. change
4. jawbone
5. jacket
6. giant
7. pencil
8. circle
9. once
10. large
11. dance
12. jeans
13. bounce
14. huge

Review

nice
place

Challenge

excited
gigantic

Write the misspelled words correctly on the lines below.

1. ____________ 6. ____________
2. ____________ 7. ____________
3. ____________ 8. ____________
4. ____________ 9. ____________
5. ____________ 10. ____________

© Houghton Mifflin Harcourt Publishing Company. All rights reserved.

Name ______________________ Date ____________

Connect to Writing

Use adjectives to describe how people, places, or things are different. To compare two nouns, add *-er* to most adjectives. To compare more than two nouns, add *-est* to most adjectives.

Compare Two	Compare More Than Two
This bone is older than that one.	This is the oldest bone we have found.
It is hotter today than yesterday.	We went digging on the hottest day of the week.

Use the correct form of the adjective in parentheses. Write the sentence.

1. *Tyrannosaurus Rex* was (big) than *Albertosaurus.*

____

2. The (long) dinosaur measured more than 100 feet in length.

____

3. Sauropod eggs are (thick) than chicken eggs.

____

4. One of the (large) dinosaur eggs was found in China.

____

© Houghton Mifflin Harcourt Publishing Company. All rights reserved.

Name ______________________ Date ____________

Words with /k/ and /kw/

Read each sentence. Choose the missing word from the box. Write the word. Then reread the complete sentence.

croaking	music	squeal
jacket	quiet	joke
squirrel	sock	tractor

1. Kim told a silly ______________ that made us all giggle.
2. It is cold outside, so wear a warm ______________.
3. After everyone went to bed, the house was very ______________.
4. My brother's band plays loud ______________.
5. "Here is my shoe, but where is my ______________?" Ana asked.
6. We saw a ______________ in a tree at the park.
7. Mr. Martin got a new ______________ for his farm.
8. The scared little pig let out a loud ______________.
9. You can hear frogs ______________ down by the pond.

© Houghton Mifflin Harcourt Publishing Company. All rights reserved.

Name ______________________ Date ____________

The Verb *be*

A Tree Is Growing
Grammar:
Using the Verb *be* and Helping Verbs

The verb *be* has different forms. Different subjects use these different forms. *Am*, *is*, and *are* show present tense. *Was* and *were* show past tense.

Ms. Greene was our teacher last year.

We were interested in her book on deserts.

One large desert is in Africa.

Thinking Question
What is the subject, and do I want to show present tense or past tense?

Choose the correct verb in ( ), and write it on the line.

1. My science project (am, is) finished. ____________
2. Ms. Burns (was, were) happy that I finished. ____________
3. Leaves (was, were) part of my project. ____________
4. They (was, were) very colorful. ____________
5. Mike's project (is, are) also finished. ____________
6. Forest animals (is, are) in his project. ____________
7. They (was, were) fun for him to draw. ____________
8. We (am, are) proud of our projects. ____________
9. The projects (is, are) on a table. ____________
10. Our room (is, are) ready for Parent Night. ____________

© Houghton Mifflin Harcourt Publishing Company. All rights reserved.

Name ______________________ Date __________

Helping Verbs

A Tree Is Growing
Grammar:
Using the Verb *be* and Helping Verbs

Helping verbs work with the main verb to help show time. Singular and plural subjects use different forms.

Subject	Helping Verbs
Singular nouns Pronouns: he, she, it	is, was, has
Plural nouns Prounouns: you, we, they	are, have, were
Pronoun: I	am, was, have

The tree was growing taller.
It has grown many branches.

The two friends were talking quietly.
We have tried to count the leaves.
They are blowing in the wind.

I am going to stop counting.
I was excited about the falling leaves.

Thinking Questions
Is the subject of the sentence singular or plural? If it is a pronoun, what form of helping verb does it take?

Write the correct verb in ( ) to complete the sentence.

1. Those workers (is, are) planting trees in the park. ____________
2. My brother (is, are) helping the workers. ____________
3. He (has, have) asked me to come with him. ____________
4. I (am, is) going to walk with them. ____________
5. One tree's leaves (has, have) already turned brown. ____________
6. Some squirrels (was, were) collecting acorns. ____________

© Houghton Mifflin Harcourt Publishing Company. All rights reserved.

Name ______________________ Date ____________

Spelling the /k/ and /kw/ Sounds

Write each Basic Word where it belongs in the chart.

kite	trick
____	____
____	____
	____

camp	quack
____	____
____	____
____	____
____	____
____	____
____	____

Challenge: Add the Challenge Words to your Word Sort.

Spelling Words

Basic

1. shark
2. check
3. queen
4. circus
5. flake
6. crack
7. second
8. squeeze
9. quart
10. squeak
11. quick
12. coldest
13. Africa
14. Mexico

Review

black
thank

Challenge

correct
question

© Houghton Mifflin Harcourt Publishing Company. All rights reserved.

Name ______________________ Date ____________

Focus Trait: Word Choice

Exact Words

Good writers of persuasive problem-and-solution paragraphs use exact words—nouns, adjectives, adverbs, and verbs—to express clearly what they want to say. Compare a sentence without exact words and a sentence with exact words.

Without Exact Words: The dog chased the cat.

With Exact words: The large, playful golden retriever chased the tiny calico cat.

Rewrite each sentence, adding exact words to express the writer's thoughts more clearly. Make up your own specific details and exact words.

1. The piano fell.

____

____

2. The puppy tripped.

____

3. The store manager told me to leave.

____

4. From the window, you can see many things.

____

____

5. The food was great.

____

© Houghton Mifflin Harcourt Publishing Company. All rights reserved.

Name ________________________ Date ____________

Cumulative Review

Write a word from the box to complete each sentence about one family's love for the zoo. Then read the complete sentence.

complain	kiss	quality
exchange	monkey	question
instead	pick	surprise

1. I have never heard anyone ________________ about our local zoo.
2. It isn't a huge zoo, but its ________________ is very good.
3. Our zookeepers have managed to ________________ animals with zoos in faraway places.
4. My favorite animal is a ________________ from India.
5. He likes to blow you a ________________ when you visit his exhibit.
6. My little brother would ________________ the zebra as his favorite animal.
7. It's probably no ________________ that my sister likes the koalas best.
8. Our family would choose a visit to the zoo ________________ of almost any other form of entertainment.
9. We all often ask the ________________, "Can we go to the zoo this weekend?"

© Houghton Mifflin Harcourt Publishing Company. All rights reserved.

Name ______________________ Date ________

Reader's Guide

A Tree Is Growing

Label a Growing Tree

What did you learn about trees? Use the features in *A Tree Is Growing* to help you draw and label a growing tree.

Read pages 94–96. Draw and label three different leaves. Write a caption telling what leaves do for trees.

____

____

____

Read pages 97–99. What is sap? What is special about some kinds of sap? Use the captions to find some of this information.

____

____

____

© Houghton Mifflin Harcourt Publishing Company. All rights reserved.

Name ________________________ Date ________

A Tree Is Growing
Independent Reading

Read pages 100–101. What are some important things about a tree's roots?

____

____

Read pages 102–105. What are some important things about a tree's bark?

____

____

Now draw a picture of your own growing tree. Use the information from the text and illustrations to label your tree's parts.

© Houghton Mifflin Harcourt Publishing Company. All rights reserved.

Name ______________________ Date __________

A Tree Is Growing
Grammar:
Using the Verb *be* and Helping Verbs

Using Verbs

Choose the correct verb in ( ), and write it on the line.

1. The pine tree (is, are) the tallest tree in the woods. ______________
2. The lakes in our state (is, are) very pretty. ______________
3. The Hudson River (is, am) the longest river in New York State. ______________
4. Our trip to Lake Erie (was, were) interesting. ______________
5. We (was, were) happy viewing the lake. ______________

Write *has* or *have* to complete each sentence correctly.

6. We ______________ read books about the ocean.
7. Jack ______________ written a report on rivers.
8. My friends ______________ worked hard on their desert project.
9. The librarian ______________ shown me books on mountains.
10. I ______________ found pictures of tall mountains for my report.

© Houghton Mifflin Harcourt Publishing Company. All rights reserved.

Name ______________________ Date ____________

Spelling the /k/ and /kw/ Sounds

Write the Basic Word that best replaces the underlined word or words in each sentence.

1. The recipe called for four cups of milk.
2. The mouse let out a high, little sound and then ran away.
3. The little piece of snow melted as soon as it touched my warm skin.
4. This is the chilliest winter day we have had this year.
5. Will you look over my report for spelling mistakes?
6. We have tickets to go to the fun show in the big tent!
7. With one fast kick, the player scored the winning goal.
8. When the king died, the king's wife became the country's leader.
9. Hold the egg carefully so that it won't break open.
10. My baby sister likes to grab my finger and hold tightly to it.

1. ____________ 6. ____________

2. ____________ 7. ____________

3. ____________ 8. ____________

4. ____________ 9. ____________

5. ____________ 10. ____________

Spelling Words

Basic

1. shark
2. check
3. queen
4. circus
5. flake
6. crack
7. second
8. squeeze
9. quart
10. squeak
11. quick
12. coldest
13. Africa
14. Mexico

Review

black
thank

Challenge

correct
question

Challenge: On a separate sheet of paper, write a sentence using each Challenge Word. Then rewrite your sentences replacing each Challenge Word with a synonym. Use a dictionary or thesaurus if you need help.

© Houghton Mifflin Harcourt Publishing Company. All rights reserved.

Name ______________________ Date ____________

Word Roots

A Tree Is Growing
Vocabulary Strategies:
Word Roots

Identify the root and tell its meaning. Use the meaning of the root to figure out the meaning of the word.

1. telephone
Root:
Meaning of the root:
Meaning of the word:

2. telescope
Root:
Meaning of the root:
Meaning of the word:

3. autocorrect
Root:
Meaning of the root:
Meaning of the word:

4. autopilot
Root:
Meaning of the root:
Meaning of the word:

5. automatic
Root:
Meaning of the root:
Meaning of the word:

© Houghton Mifflin Harcourt Publishing Company. All rights reserved.

Name ____________________ Date ____________

Abstract Nouns

A Tree Is Growing
Grammar:
Spiral Review

- Nouns are words that name people, places, or things.
- **Abstract nouns** name things that *cannot* be seen, touched, heard, smelled, or tasted.

idea energy growth happiness

Mira had a good idea about saving energy.

The growth of my plants fills me with happiness.

Thinking Question
Can I see, touch, hear, smell, or taste it?

Write the abstract noun in each sentence.

1. Fear stopped him from opening the door. ____________
2. Ben's disappointment made him very quiet. ____________
3. The puppy barked with joy. ____________
4. Jan had the freedom to pick her own books. ____________
5. Jill was filled with relief when she found her lost hamster.

____

© Houghton Mifflin Harcourt Publishing Company. All rights reserved.

Name ______________________ Date ____________

Proofreading for Spelling

A Tree Is Growing
Spelling:
Spelling the /k/ and /kw/ Sounds

Find the misspelled words and circle them.

Dear Sam,

I am having a great time in Mexico. On the seckond day of our trip, Dad took me snorkeling. I had to wear a wetsuit because the water here is the koldest I've ever felt! Before we got in the water, Dad called the beach patrol to ask a very important qwestion. He had to chek and make sure there was no sharck danger!

Snorkeling was fun. We saw all kinds of fish. I even saw one called a clownfish. It was as colorful as a real circkus clown! Dad pointed out a fish trying to catch a little squid. We watched the squid scueeze out black ink. Then it made a quik getaway. It was amazing to see!

Today my parents and I went to the market. We used some of the Spanish words we've learned. People smile and try to understand us even when we don't say things the korrect way. Sometimes we get the words all mixed up and just crac up laughing.

We are having a lot of fun. I hope you are having fun back at home. I'll see you in a few days.

Your friend,
Mark

Spelling Words

Basic

1. shark
2. check
3. queen
4. circus
5. flake
6. crack
7. second
8. squeeze
9. quart
10. squeak
11. quick
12. coldest
13. Africa
14. Mexico

Review

black
thank

Challenge

correct
question

On a separate sheet of paper, write the misspelled words correctly.

© Houghton Mifflin Harcourt Publishing Company. All rights reserved.

Name ______________________ Date ____________

Connect to Writing

Short Sentences	Longer, Smoother Sentence
Mount Whitney is very high. White Mountain is very high.	Mount Whitney and White Mountain are very high.
Elise has hiked in the woods. Jamik has hiked in the woods.	Elise and Jamik have hiked in the woods.

Combine two short sentences by moving one subject to make one longer sentence with two subjects. Write the new sentence on the line. Be sure to change the forms of the verbs to match the subject of the new sentence.

1. A goat lives in the mountains. A wolf lives in the mountains.

____

2. A hiker has stopped at the ranger station. A camper has stopped at the ranger station.

____

3. My aunt likes hiking in the woods. My uncle likes hiking in the woods.

____

4. Ellen has reached the top of the mountain. Steven has reached the top of the mountain.

____

5. Ali was on the bridge. Jane was on the bridge.

____

© Houghton Mifflin Harcourt Publishing Company. All rights reserved.

Name ______________________________ Date ____________

Vowel Sounds in *spoon* and *wood*

Read each sentence. Choose the missing word from the box. Write the word. Then reread the complete sentence.

hooded	juicy	screws
sunroof	reduce	shouldn't
clue	youth	rules

1. Max hid a present for his mother and left a very good ______________ about where to look for it.

2. To help the environment, we are trying to ______________ the amount of trash we create.

3. We should use ______________, not nails, to put the birdhouse together.

4. The large dog stuck his head out the ______________ when his owner took him for a ride in the sports car.

5. My grandfather likes to tell stories about what life was like in his ______________.

6. Before the game, the umpire reminded us to play by the ______________.

7. You ______________ run when the sidewalk is slippery.

8. Dad told me to wear my ______________ jacket to keep my ears warm.

9. The ______________ watermelon dripped on my shirt.

© Houghton Mifflin Harcourt Publishing Company. All rights reserved.

Come, Do, Go, Run, and *See*

The verbs **come**, **do**, **go**, **run**, and **see** are irregular and have special spellings to show past tense. These verbs may also have other spellings when they are used with *has*, *had*, or *have*.

A mouse had gone into our house.

The mouse ran into the woods yesterday.

Thinking Questions
Is the verb in the past tense? Is the verb used with has, have, *or* had?

Write the correct past tense of the verb in parentheses to complete each sentence.

1. My sister had (went, gone) outside. ______________
2. Tammy (saw, seen) the mouse in a pile of leaves. ______________
3. My brother has (ran, run) outside, too. ______________
4. Our neighbors had (saw, seen) the mouse on the bird feeder.

   ____
5. The mice also (did, done) some damage to some feed bags.

   ____
6. They have (ran, run) through the gardens. ______________
7. The baby mice (go, went) into the nest. ______________
8. I (did, done) a drawing of a mouse last night.

   ____

© Houghton Mifflin Harcourt Publishing Company. All rights reserved.

Name ______________________ Date ____________

Eat, Give, Grow, Take, and *Write*

The verbs **eat**, **give**, **grow**, **take**, and **write** have special spellings to show past tense. These verbs also have other spellings when they are used with *has*, *had*, and *have*.

My mother gave me a book about bears.

The author has written books about other animals.

Thinking Questions
Is the verb in the past tense? Is the verb used with has, have, *or* had?

Write the correct past tense of the verb in parentheses to complete each sentence.

1. I (wrote, written) my name on the cover of my book. ______________
2. The first chapter (gave, given) facts about bears. ______________
3. I have (took, taken) the book to my friend's house. ______________
4. She (gave, given) me a book about mountain lions. ______________
5. She had (wrote, written) her name in her book, too. ______________
6. Her dog had (ate, eaten) a corner of the book. ______________
7. That dog has (grew, grown) a lot this year! ______________
8. I (ate, eaten) a cookie before leaving. ______________

© Houghton Mifflin Harcourt Publishing Company. All rights reserved.

Name ____________________ Date __________

Vowel Sounds in *spoon* and *wood*

Two Bear Cubs
Spelling:
Vowel Sounds in *spoon* and *wood*

Write each Basic Word under the correct heading.

Vowel Sounds in *spoon*	Vowel Sounds in *wood*
____________	____________
____________	____________
____________	____________
____________	____________
____________	____________
____________	____________
____________	____________
____________	____________
____________	____________
____________	____________
____________	____________
____________	____________
____________	____________
____________	____________
____________	____________

Spelling Words

Basic

1. mood
2. wooden
3. drew
4. smooth
5. blue
6. balloon
7. true
8. crooked
9. chew
10. tooth
11. hooves
12. cool
13. food
14. pooch

Review

blew
foot

Challenge

loose
jewel

Challenge: Add the Challenge Words to your Word Sort.

© Houghton Mifflin Harcourt Publishing Company. All rights reserved.

Name ______________________ Date ____________

Focus Trait: Ideas

Thinking About Your Audience

Good writers ask, "What reasons will convince my audience to agree with me?"

Marla is writing to convince her parents to let her go on a class trip to the zoo. Marla brainstormed reasons. Then she chose the ones that her audience, her parents, would care most about.

- She can learn many things about animals, such as bears, at the zoo.
- The teacher, principal, and five other parents will be on the trip.
- She will promise to follow safety rules.

Read about each writer and his or her goal. Underline the reason that the writer's audience would care most about. Then add another reason that the audience would care about.

1. Jovan is writing to convince his older brother to follow their mother's rules.

A. When we follow Mother's rules, she is happier.

B. Mother likes to go to the gym in the afternoons while we are at school.

Another reason: ______________________________

2. Stephanie is writing to convince her father to let her join the soccer team.

A. Soccer is one of the most popular sports in the world.

B. Soccer is great exercise, and lots of players make new friends.

Another reason: ______________________________

© Houghton Mifflin Harcourt Publishing Company. All rights reserved.

Name ____________________ Date __________

Two Bear Cubs
Phonics:
Cumulative Review

Cumulative Review

Choose a word from the box to complete each sentence. Write the word on the line. Then read the sentence.

shampoo	woof	lookout
chewing	clues	food

1. In comic strips, dogs often say "arf" or "______________."
2. To keep its owner safe, a guide dog is always on the ______________.
3. Some dogs use their noses to find ______________ about the right trail to follow.
4. Most grown dogs eat twice a day, but puppies need ______________ four times a day.
5. Dogs should be washed with ______________ made just for dogs. Try not to get the suds in the dog's eyes.
6. Sometimes a dog enjoys ______________ on a special treat to keep its teeth healthy and strong.

© Houghton Mifflin Harcourt Publishing Company. All rights reserved.

Name ______________________________ Date ______

Reader's Guide

Two Bear Cubs

Write a Theater Review

Write a review of *Two Bear Cubs* for your local newspaper. First, use details from the text and illustrations to gather information about the play.

Read pages 134–136. Describe the setting and main characters.

____

____

Read page 137. How does the end of Scene 1 change the story?

____

____

Read pages 139–143. What happens in Scene 2? How does it end?

____

____

Read pages 145–149. Who is the hero of Scene 3? Why?

____

____

Read page 151. What is the message at the very end of the play?

____

____

© Houghton Mifflin Harcourt Publishing Company. All rights reserved.

Name ____________________ Date ________

Now use all the details from the previous page to write your review. Include the characters, the setting, and the plot. At the end, be sure to say whether you like the play and why.

A Review of *Two Bear Cubs*

© Houghton Mifflin Harcourt Publishing Company. All rights reserved.

Name ________________________ Date ____________

Come, Do, Go, Run, See, Eat, Give, Grow, Take, and *Write*

Write the correct past tense of the verb in parentheses to complete each sentence.

1. The class (go, went) to the play downtown. ____________
2. Some parents (come, came) with us last year. ____________
3. The actors have (grow, grown) stronger since last year. ____________
4. One person (took, taken) her camera to the play. ____________
5. We have (wrote, written) about the play for class. ____________

Write the correct past-tense form of the verb in parentheses to complete the sentence.

6. In the play, actors ____________ their best to please the crowd. (do)
7. The actors pretended to have ____________ a huge feast. (eat)
8. A friend ____________ to my seat during the play. (come)
9. He ____________ a few pictures with his camera. (take)
10. We have ____________ some interesting plays this year. (see)

© Houghton Mifflin Harcourt Publishing Company. All rights reserved.

Name ______________________ Date ____________

Vowel Sounds in *spoon* and *wood*

Use the Basic Words to complete the puzzle.

Spelling Words

Basic

1. mood
2. wooden
3. drew
4. smooth
5. blue
6. balloon
7. true
8. crooked
9. chew
10. tooth
11. hooves
12. cool
13. food
14. pooch

Review

blew
foot

Challenge

loose
jewel

Across

2. used to bite
3. to eat
7. not straight
8. what you eat
10. It is filled with air.

Down

1. small dog
4. made of boards
5. traced or sketched
6. opposite of warm
9. feeling

© Houghton Mifflin Harcourt Publishing Company. All rights reserved.

Name ______________________ Date ____________

Prefixes *pre-*, *re-*, *bi-*

In each sentence, circle the word with the prefix *pre-*, *re-*, or *bi-*. Then write the base word, the prefix, and the word meaning.

1. My mom can fix just about anything that goes wrong on a bicycle.

______________ ______________ ______________
base word **prefix** **meaning**

2. I always go get popcorn during the previews at the movies.

______________ ______________ ______________
base word **prefix** **meaning**

3. Jenna liked the book so much that she reread it three times.

______________ ______________ ______________
base word **prefix** **meaning**

4. Hector and I meet biweekly to work on our social studies project.

______________ ______________ ______________
base word **prefix** **meaning**

5. Our class visited a museum to see an exhibit of prehistoric art.

______________ ______________ ______________
base word **prefix** **meaning**

© Houghton Mifflin Harcourt Publishing Company. All rights reserved.

Name ______________________ Date __________

Pronoun-Verb Agreement

- Add *-s* or *-es* to a verb in the present tense when the pronoun in the subject is *he*, *she*, or *it*.
- Do not add *-s* or *-es* to a verb in the present tense when the pronoun in the subject is *I*, *you*, *we*, or *they*.
- Change the *y* to *i* and add *-es* to form the present tense of verbs that end with *y* when the subject is *he*, *she*, or *it*.

I toss the ball. I fly kites.

She splashes into the lake. She flies kites.

Write the correct verb in parentheses to go with each underlined subject.

1. He (drive, drives) to the theater. ______________
2. We (watch, watches) the actors. ______________
3. They (perform, performs) really well. ______________
4. She (study, studies) acting. ______________

Combine each pair of sentences. Change the underlined words to pronouns. Write the new sentences on the lines.

5. Aunt Clara goes to plays. Aunt Clara goes to concerts, too.

____

6. A bus takes them to the theater. A bus brings them back, too.

____

© Houghton Mifflin Harcourt Publishing Company. All rights reserved.

Name ______________________ Date ____________

Two Bear Cubs
Spelling:
Vowel Sounds in *spoon* and *wood*

Proofreading for Spelling

Find and circle the misspelled words.

Dear Grandma,

Thank you for the wonderful day at the petting zoo. It put me in such a good moud. I remember hearing hooves as we walked across the wuden bridge. Seeing a mule up close was cule! I liked feeding it hay to chue.

It was fun to feed the animals handfuls of their special fuud. I liked petting the deer's smoath fur. I think the lamb smiled at me. It had a cute crooked tooth!

I really like the blue ballone you got me. It reminds me of our fun day. I droo a picture that I am sending to you. It shows you, me, the lamb, the mule, and the black pooch we saw. It is true that this day was the best one ever!

Love,
Quinn

Spelling Words

Basic
1. mood
2. wooden
3. drew
4. smooth
5. blue
6. balloon
7. true
8. crooked
9. chew
10. tooth
11. hooves
12. cool
13. food
14. pooch

Review
blew
foot

Challenge
loose
jewel

Write the misspelled words correctly on the lines below.

1. ____________ 5. ____________
2. ____________ 6. ____________
3. ____________ 7. ____________
4. ____________ 8. ____________

© Houghton Mifflin Harcourt Publishing Company. All rights reserved.

Name ______________________ Date ____________

Connect to Writing

Using exact verbs helps the reader better picture what you are describing in your writing.

Less Exact Verb	More Exact Verb
run	sprint, jog, dash, race
talk	whisper, chatter, gossip, debate

For each verb, write a sentence that shows its exact meaning. Use a dictionary if you need help.

1. sprint

____

____

2. jog

____

____

3. dash

____

____

4. race

____

____

5. whisper

____

____

© Houghton Mifflin Harcourt Publishing Company. All rights reserved.

Name ______________________ Date ____________

Compound Words

Write a word from the box to answer each clue. Then answer the question below by reading the word in the shaded boxes.

chalkboard	flashlight	outside	toothbrush
cookbook	homework	snowshoes	underwater
fireplace	newspaper		

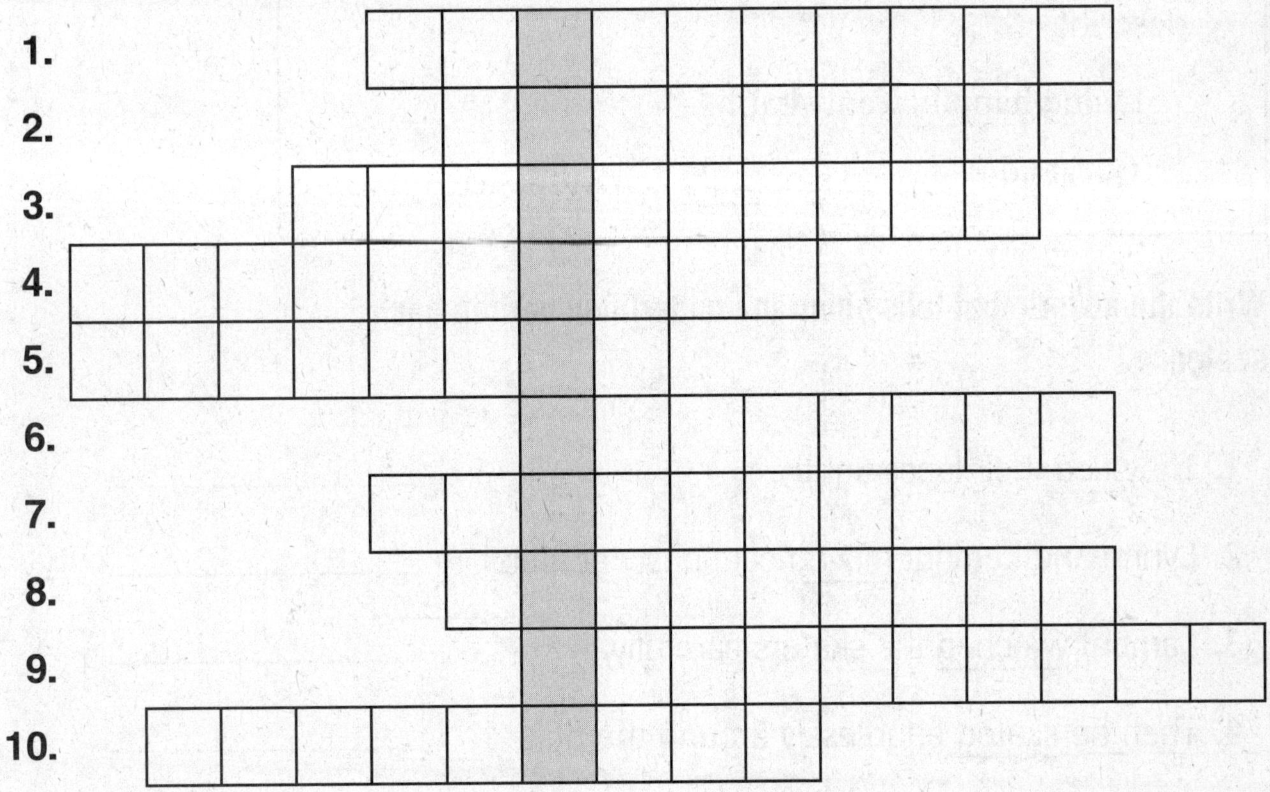

1. This helps you see in the dark.
2. You wear these to walk in snow.
3. You need this to brush your teeth.
4. Look here to see fish in a lake.
5. You do this work after school.
6. This is a book of recipes.
7. You might play here after school.
8. A fire in here will warm a room.
9. A teacher may write on this in a classroom.
10. You read this to learn the news.

What is the coldest place on Earth? ____________________

© Houghton Mifflin Harcourt Publishing Company. All rights reserved.

Name ______________________ Date ____________

Adverbs That Tell *How*

Life on the Ice
Grammar:
What Is an Adverb?

- Words that describe verbs are called **adverbs**.
- Adverbs can tell *how* an action happens. Most adverbs that tell *how* end in *-ly*.
- Adverbs can come before or after the verbs they describe.

Lynne happily went skating.

The skaters moved smoothly across the ice.

Thinking Question
What word tells how?

Write the adverb that tells about the underlined verb in each sentence.

1. They tied their laces tightly. ____________
2. Lynne and Lamont moved cautiously at first. ____________
3. Lamont watched the skaters carefully. ____________
4. Then he skated effortlessly around the rink. ____________
5. Proudly, Lynne spun on the ice. ____________
6. Lynne's lace broke unexpectedly. ____________
7. Slowly, she moved to a bench. ____________
8. She arrived at the bench safely. ____________

© Houghton Mifflin Harcourt Publishing Company. All rights reserved.

Name ______________________ Date ____________

Adverbs That Tell *Where* and *When*

- **Adverbs** can tell *how* an action happens. They can also tell *where* and *when* something happens.
- Adverbs can come before or after the verbs they describe.

The scientists flew there in an airplane.

Then they cleaned the airplane.

Thinking Question
What word tells where or when?

Write the adverb that tells about each underlined verb. Then write *where* or *when* to show how each adverb describes the verb.

1. It's too snowy to leave tonight. ____________
2. First, we will make a shelter. ____________
3. Then we will drink hot chocolate. ____________
4. We can build a shelter there. ____________
5. We will ride snowmobiles tomorrow. ____________
6. We can skate nearby. ____________
7. They hiked away, but then they came back. ____________
8. The iceberg lies ahead. ____________

© Houghton Mifflin Harcourt Publishing Company. All rights reserved.

Name ____________________ Date __________

Life on the Ice
Spelling:
Compound Words

Spelling Word Sort

Read each Basic Word. Listen to the number of syllables. Write each word under the correct heading.

Words with Two Syllables	Words with Three Syllables
________	________
________	________
________	________
________	________
________	________
________	________
________	________
________	________
________	________
________	________
________	________

Review: **Add the Review Words to your Word Sort.**

Challenge: Which Challenge Word has four syllables?

____

Add the other Challenge Word to your Word Sort.

Spelling Words

Basic

1. birthday
2. anyone
3. sometimes
4. everything
5. homework
6. afternoon
7. airplane
8. grandmother
9. something
10. without
11. himself
12. faraway
13. sunburned
14. daylight

Review

someone
cannot

Challenge

scorekeeper
everybody

© Houghton Mifflin Harcourt Publishing Company. All rights reserved.

Name _______________ Date _______________

Life on the Ice
Writing:
Opinion Writing

Focus Trait: Organization

Paragraphs for Reasons

Good writers make a separate paragraph for each reason in a persuasive essay.

Reasons Together	***Reasons in Paragraphs***
In Antarctica, scientists can learn about pollution. For example, they can find ash from Mount Vesuvius. They learn about how the climate is changing. They can see how quickly icc is melting.	In Antarctica, scientists can learn about pollution. For example, they can find ash from Mount Vesuvius. Additionally, they learn about how the climate is changing. They can see how quickly ice is melting.

Rewrite the following paragraph so that each reason has its own paragraph. Add linking words between paragraphs.

A century ago, explorers built huts in Antarctica. Today, the huts are falling apart. We should save the huts because they are an important part of history. The huts are full of food and clothing. These items can teach us what the explorers' lives were like. The huts are full of books. By reading them, we can learn how explorers prepared for their trip.

© Houghton Mifflin Harcourt Publishing Company. All rights reserved.

Name ______________________ Date __________

Cumulative Review

Read each sentence. Choose two words from the Word Bank to form a compound word to complete each sentence. Then read the complete sentence.

bare	brush	eye	sun
bath	brow	fire	room
boat	butter	fly	sail
glasses	camp	foot	paint

1. When you do not have a shoe or sock on your foot, you are ________________.
2. You use ________________ to protect your eyes.
3. To make a colorful picture, you use a ________________.
4. The hair that grows just above your eye is called an ________________.
5. You take a shower in a room called a ________________.
6. An insect that uses its pretty wings to fly from flower to flower is called a ________________.
7. A boat that uses wind and sails is called a ________________.
8. When you want to cook something while you are camping, you build a ________________.

© Houghton Mifflin Harcourt Publishing Company. All rights reserved.

Name ______________________ Date ______

Reader's Guide

Life on the Ice

A Travel Guide to the Poles

Gather information about the North and South Poles. Use the information to create a travel guide.

Read pages 170–171. Where are the Poles? What are they like?

____

____

Read pages 174–175. What is traveling to the Poles like?

____

____

Read pages 180–181. How do you need to dress at the Poles?

____

____

Read pages 182–183. What are the different seasons like for people who live at the Poles?

____

____

© Houghton Mifflin Harcourt Publishing Company. All rights reserved.

Name ______________________ Date ______

Life on the Ice
Independent Reading

Now use the information you collected to design a travel guide for the North and South Poles. Be sure to point out interesting details that would make visitors eager to go. Remember to let your excitement show!

Come to the North and South Poles! An adventure awaits you!

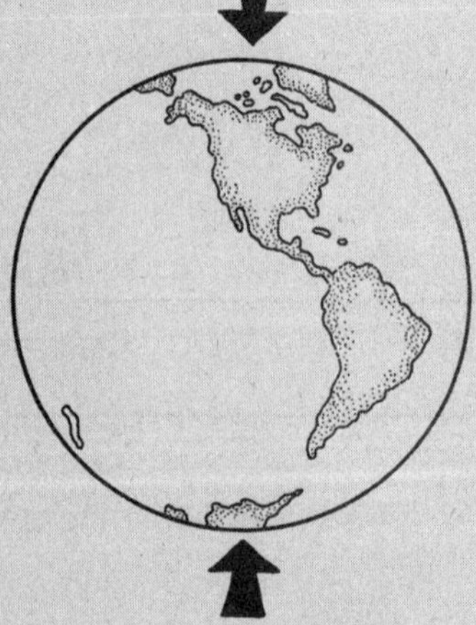

© Houghton Mifflin Harcourt Publishing Company. All rights reserved.

Name ______________________ Date ____________

Adverbs That Tell *How*, *Where*, and *When*

Write the adverb that tells *how* the underlined verb happened.

1. The airplane noisily landed on the runway. ____________
2. The engines roared loudly as we waited. ____________
3. Cheerfully, we waved at the scientists. ____________
4. The pilots sternly nodded at us. ____________

Write the adverb that describes the underlined verb. Then write *where* or *when* to show how each adverb describes the verb.

5. First, we showed the scientists their rooms. ____________
6. We talked with them inside. ____________
7. We walked upstairs for a snack. ____________
8. Another group arrives tomorrow. ____________

© Houghton Mifflin Harcourt Publishing Company. All rights reserved.

Name ____________________ Date __________

Spelling Compound Words

Life on the Ice
Spelling:
Compound Words

Read each book title. Add a Basic Word to complete each title.

1. *Teacher, My Dog Ate My* ______________!
2. *Using Sunblock to Avoid Getting* ______________
3. *Happy* ______________*, Rosalinda!*
4. *Sixteen Hours of* ______________
5. *Traveling in an* ______________
6. *Scott's* ______________ *Pen Pal*
7. *Spending the Summer with* ______________ *and Grandpa*
8. *An* ______________ *at the Zoo*
9. *In the Rain* ______________ *an Umbrella*
10. Does ______________ *Know What Time It Is?*

Review: **Choose a Review Word. Use it in a book title.**

____

Challenge: **Choose a Challenge Word. Use it in a book title.**

____

Spelling Words

Basic

1. birthday
2. anyone
3. sometimes
4. everything
5. homework
6. afternoon
7. airplane
8. grandmother
9. something
10. without
11. himself
12. faraway
13. sunburned
14. daylight

Review

someone
cannot

Challenge

scorekeeper
everybody

© Houghton Mifflin Harcourt Publishing Company. All rights reserved.

Name ______________________ Date ____________

Dictionary/Glossary

Life on the Ice
Vocabulary Strategies:
Dictionary/Glossary

Read each word. Write the base word to use to find its dictionary entry. Then find each entry word in a dictionary. Write the words with all their endings.

Word	Entry Word in Dictionary	Part(s) of Speech	Word with Endings
1. gliding			
2. hesitate			
3. dripping			
4. rippling			
5. horrifying			

Now write a sentence for one form of each word.

1. ____

____

2. ____

____

3. ____

____

4. ____

____

5. ____

____

© Houghton Mifflin Harcourt Publishing Company. All rights reserved.

Name ______________________ Date ____________

Simple Verb Tenses

- A verb that tells about an action that has already happened shows **past tense.** Add *-ed* to most verbs to show past tense.
- A verb that tells about an action happening now shows **present tense.** Add *-s* to the verb when the noun in the subject of a sentence is singular. Do not add *-s* to the verb when the noun in the subject is *I, you,* or a plural.
- A verb that tells about an action that will happen in the future shows **future tense.** Use the helping verb *will* for verbs in the future tense.

Write the correct past tense of the verb in parentheses.

1. They ________________ to get inside. (hurry)

2. The snow ________________ after two hours. (stop)

Write the correct present tense of the verb in parentheses.

3. The girl ________________ in the snow. (play)

4. The adults ________________ for the skaters. (clap)

Write the correct future tense of the verb in parentheses.

5. We ________________ the snow from the steps. (sweep)

6. The snow ________________ when the sun comes up. (melt)

© Houghton Mifflin Harcourt Publishing Company. All rights reserved.

Name ____________________ Date __________

Proofreading for Spelling

Life on the Ice
Spelling:
Compound Words

Read the following letter. Circle the misspelled words.

Dear Grandmoter,

Thank you for my bithday card. It came in the mail this afternown. I love everthing you send me.

I wish you didn't live in such a farawy place. Sumtimes I wish I had an airplan. I would fly to see you all the time. I could be back home when it was still daylite.

Yesterday, I came home from school and played outside. I got sunberned. I canot play outside today. I have a lot of homwork to do.

I can't say goodbye withowt saying I love you and I miss you. I hope you can come see us soon!

Love,
Tony

Spelling Words

Basic

1. birthday
2. anyone
3. sometimes
4. everything
5. homework
6. afternoon
7. airplane
8. grandmother
9. something
10. without
11. himself
12. faraway
13. sunburned
14. daylight

Review

someone
cannot

Challenge

scorekeeper
everybody

Write the misspelled words correctly on the lines below.

1. ____________ 7. ____________
2. ____________ 8. ____________
3. ____________ 9. ____________
4. ____________ 10. ____________
5. ____________ 11. ____________
6. ____________ 12. ____________

© Houghton Mifflin Harcourt Publishing Company. All rights reserved.

Name ________________________ Date ____________

Connect to Writing

Short, choppy sentences can be combined to make your writing smoother. Combine two sentences by moving an adverb.

Short Sentences	Longer, Smoother Sentences
Sam walked up the hill. The hill was nearby.	Sam walked up the nearby hill.
They wait to skate. They wait eagerly.	They wait eagerly to skate.

Combine two short, choppy sentences by moving the adverb. Write the sentence.

1. We rode our sleds. We rode today.

____

2. I screamed as I flew downhill. I screamed loudly.

____

3. I ran back up the hill. I ran eagerly.

____

4. I reached the top. I reached it first.

____

© Houghton Mifflin Harcourt Publishing Company. All rights reserved.

Name ______________________________ Date ________

Reader's Guide

Boy, Were We Wrong About Dinosaurs!

An Ancient Chinese Scroll

Imagine you were in ancient China and helped find the giant bones! You will write on a Chinese scroll to explain what you saw. First, answer some questions that will help you write about your findings.

Read pages 4–6. How were the first dinosaur bones found?

____

____

Why did wise men think the bones came from dragons?

____

____

Why didn't they know the bones came from dinosaurs?

____

____

How do you think the men in ancient China felt once they discovered the huge bones?

____

____

© Houghton Mifflin Harcourt Publishing Company. All rights reserved.

Name ____________________________ Date ________

Now use your answers to write a scroll. Tell how you found the bones. Tell what you thought they were. Tell how you felt about your find.

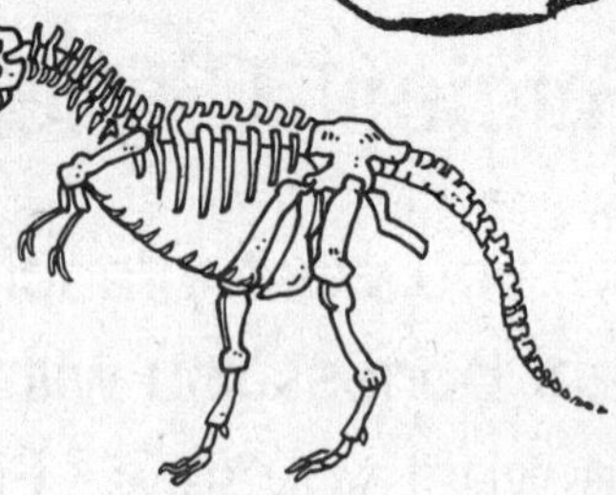

© Houghton Mifflin Harcourt Publishing Company. All rights reserved.

Name ______________________ Date ________

Then and Now Pictures

Scientists had some wrong ideas about dinosaurs! Draw pictures that show how scientists' ideas about dinosours have changed. First, use the text and illustrations to answer the questions below.

Read page 8. What did scientists first think about the horn-shaped bone of the iguanodon?

____

____

Read page 9. What did scientists realize later about the horn-shaped bone?

____

____

Read page 10. What did scientists first think about the elbows and knees of dinosaurs?

____

____

How did scientists first think that dinosaurs moved?

____

____

© Houghton Mifflin Harcourt Publishing Company. All rights reserved.

Name ______________________________ Date ________

Now use your answers to draw two pictures of an iguanadon. First, draw what scientists used to think they looked like. Next, draw what scientists now believe. Write captions to explain your drawings.

Iguanodon Then

____

____

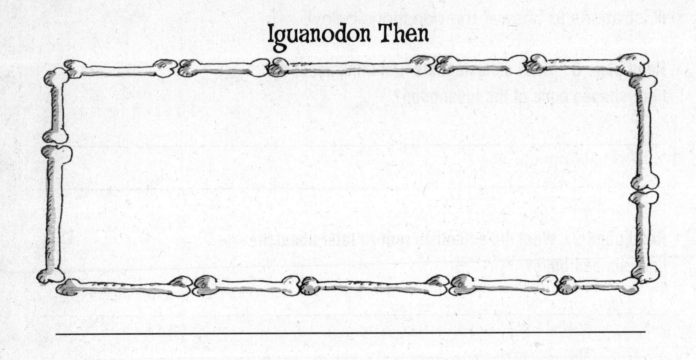

Iguanodon Now

____

____

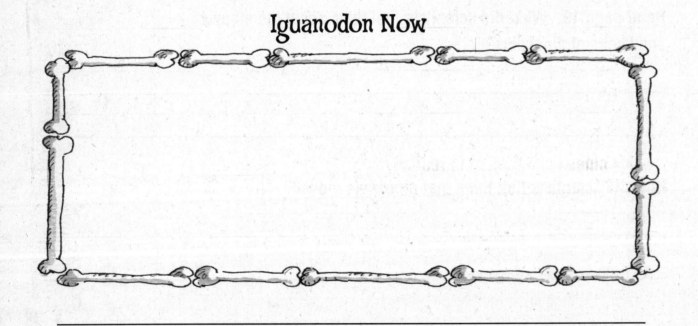

© Houghton Mifflin Harcourt Publishing Company. All rights reserved.

Name ______________________ Date ________

Now answer some questions about dinosaurs' tails. You will use your answers to draw more Then and Now pictures.

Read page 12. What did scientists think about dinosaurs' tails?

____

____

What evidence made them believe that?

____

____

____

Read page 13. Now what do scientists think that dinosaurs did with their tails?

____

____

____

What clues helped them to realize this?

____

____

____

© Houghton Mifflin Harcourt Publishing Company. All rights reserved.

Name ______________________________ Date ________

First, draw what scientists used to think about dinosaurs' tails. Next, draw what scientists now believe about their tails. Write captions to explain your drawings.

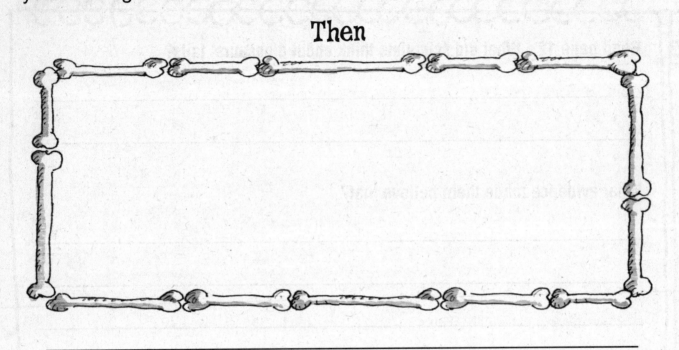

Then

____

____

Now

____

____

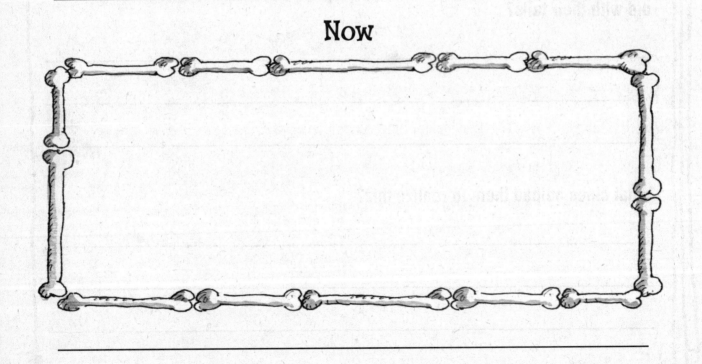

© Houghton Mifflin Harcourt Publishing Company. All rights reserved.

Name ______________________ Date ________

Reader's Guide

Boy, Were We Wrong About Dinosaurs!

A Letter to the Past

You are going to send a letter in a time machine! The letter will go to scientists who worked and lived hundreds of years ago. What will you tell them about dinosaurs? First, gather facts from the text. Then, write your letter.

Read page 14. How did scientists think dinosaurs were like lizards?

____

____

____

What do lizard bones look like inside?

____

____

____

How do dinosaur bones compare with lizard bones?

____

____

____

© Houghton Mifflin Harcourt Publishing Company. All rights reserved.

Name ______________________ Date ______

Read page 15. How do scientists think dinosaurs were like birds?

____

____

____

Read pages 16–18. Why do scientists think big dinosaurs did not have fur or feathers?

____

____

Read page 19. Why do scientists think little dinosaurs had feathers?

____

____

Read page 20. What do scientists now think about the colors of dinosaurs?

____

____

____

© Houghton Mifflin Harcourt Publishing Company. All rights reserved.

Name ______________________ Date ________

Now use this information to write a letter to scientists of the past. Explain in this letter what we now know about the bones, blood, feathers, and colors of dinosaurs.

Dear Scientists of the Past,

Sincerely yours,

© Houghton Mifflin Harcourt Publishing Company. All rights reserved.

Name ______________________________ Date ______

Look Under the Microscope

Suppose you are the leader of a group of scientists who are digging up dinosaur bones. When your group has gathered all the fossils you need, you will be looking at the fossils under a microscope. Draw and label everything you find. Then write a lab report.

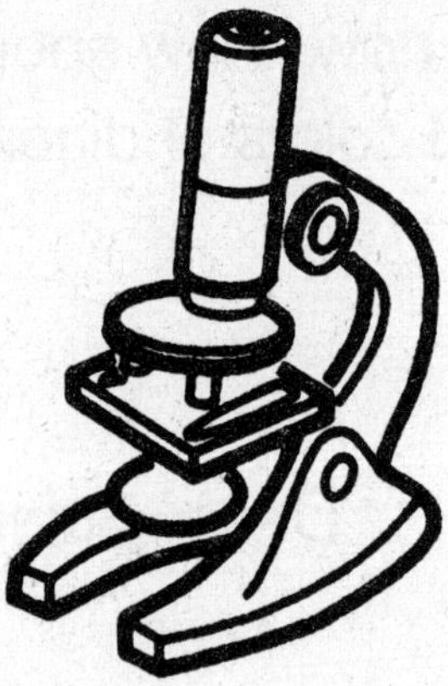

Read page 14. You have just found a dinosaur bone and sliced it open. Draw and label what you see under the microscope.

____

____

____

____

Read page 16. You have just found a fossil with some marks that look like feathers. Draw and label what you see under the microscope.

____

____

____

____

© Houghton Mifflin Harcourt Publishing Company. All rights reserved.

Name ______________________ Date ________

Read page 18. You have just found the skin of a large dinosaur. Is it smooth or bumpy? Does it have feathers or fur? Draw and label what you see under the microscope.

Read page 19. Now you have found the skin of a small dinosaur. Is it smooth or bumpy? Does it have feathers or fur? Draw and label what you see under the microscope.

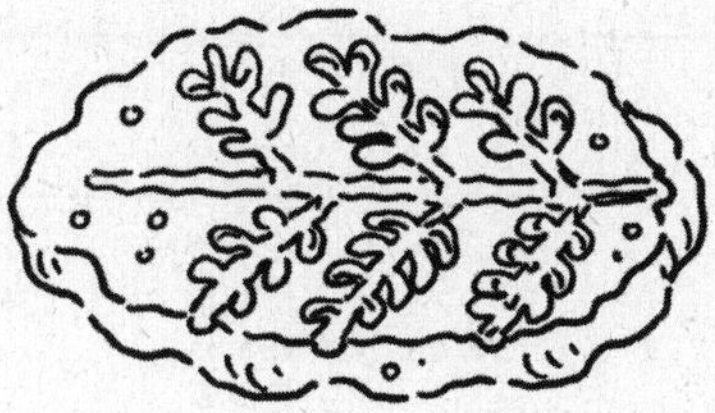

© Houghton Mifflin Harcourt Publishing Company. All rights reserved.

Name ______________________ Date ______

Now use what you saw under the microscope to write a lab report. Describe your discoveries about the different parts of dinosaurs.

Lab Report

© Houghton Mifflin Harcourt Publishing Company. All rights reserved.

Reader's Guide

Boy, Were We Wrong About Dinosaurs!

Dinosaur Short Story

After reading this book, you know a lot about baby dinosaurs! Use the text and illustrations to write a short story about a baby dinosaur. First, answer the questions below to get the main details.

Read pages 22–23. What is the same about dinosaur babies and lizard babies?

____

____

What is different about dinosaur babies and lizard babies?

____

____

____

Read page 24. What did the nests of dinosaurs tell us about them?

____

____

What did fossil footprints of dinosaurs tell us about dinosaur babies?

____

____

© Houghton Mifflin Harcourt Publishing Company. All rights reserved.

Name ______________________ Date ______

Now write your story about a baby dinosaur. You can include details about how the baby was born, how the mother took care of it, and how it traveled with its family.

© Houghton Mifflin Harcourt Publishing Company. All rights reserved.

Name ______________________ Date ________

Draw a Comic Strip

Scientist had many different ideas about what killed off the dinosaurs. Use the text and illustrations to draw a comic strip showing what you think might have happened. The questions below will help you think of some ideas.

Read page 26. What did scientists first think killed off the dinosaurs?

____

____

Why did scientists change their minds about what killed off the dinosaurs?

____

____

____

Read page 27. Why would dinosaurs die if the sun was blocked?

____

____

____

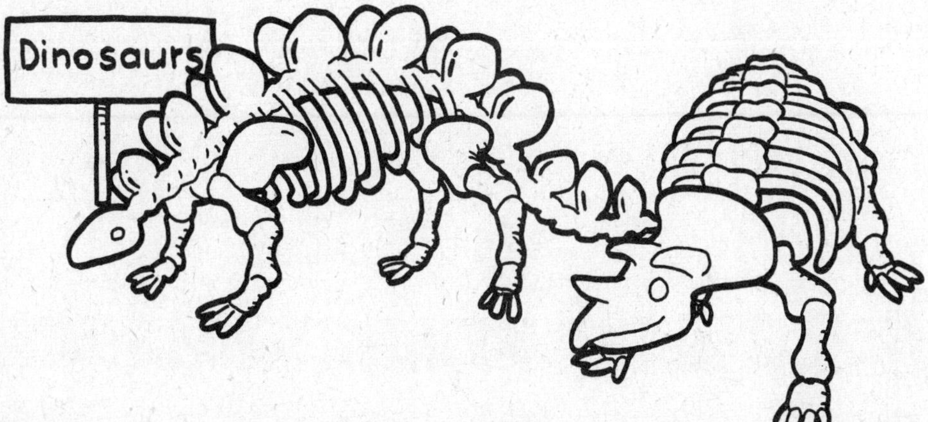

© Houghton Mifflin Harcourt Publishing Company. All rights reserved.

Name ______________________ Date ______

Now draw a comic strip showing how scientists think the dinosaurs died.

© Houghton Mifflin Harcourt Publishing Company. All rights reserved.

Name _______________________________ Date _______

Write a Speech

We may still be wrong about the dinosaurs. Scientists keep making discoveries. Be a scientist! You have just made an important discovery about dinosaurs. Plan the speech you are going to give to a group of scientists about your discovery. Then write the speech.

Read pages 22–24. What don't we know about dinosaur babies?

____

____

____

Read pages 26–27. What don't we know about why dinosaurs died?

____

____

____

Read page 29. Why do some scientists believe that some dinosaurs are still alive?

____

____

What are some other things we don't know about dinosaurs yet?

____

____

© Houghton Mifflin Harcourt Publishing Company. All rights reserved.

Name ____________________ Date ______

Now write your speech about your latest discovery. You are going to talk to a group of scientists. Describe the new information you have about dinosaurs and why you believe it is true.

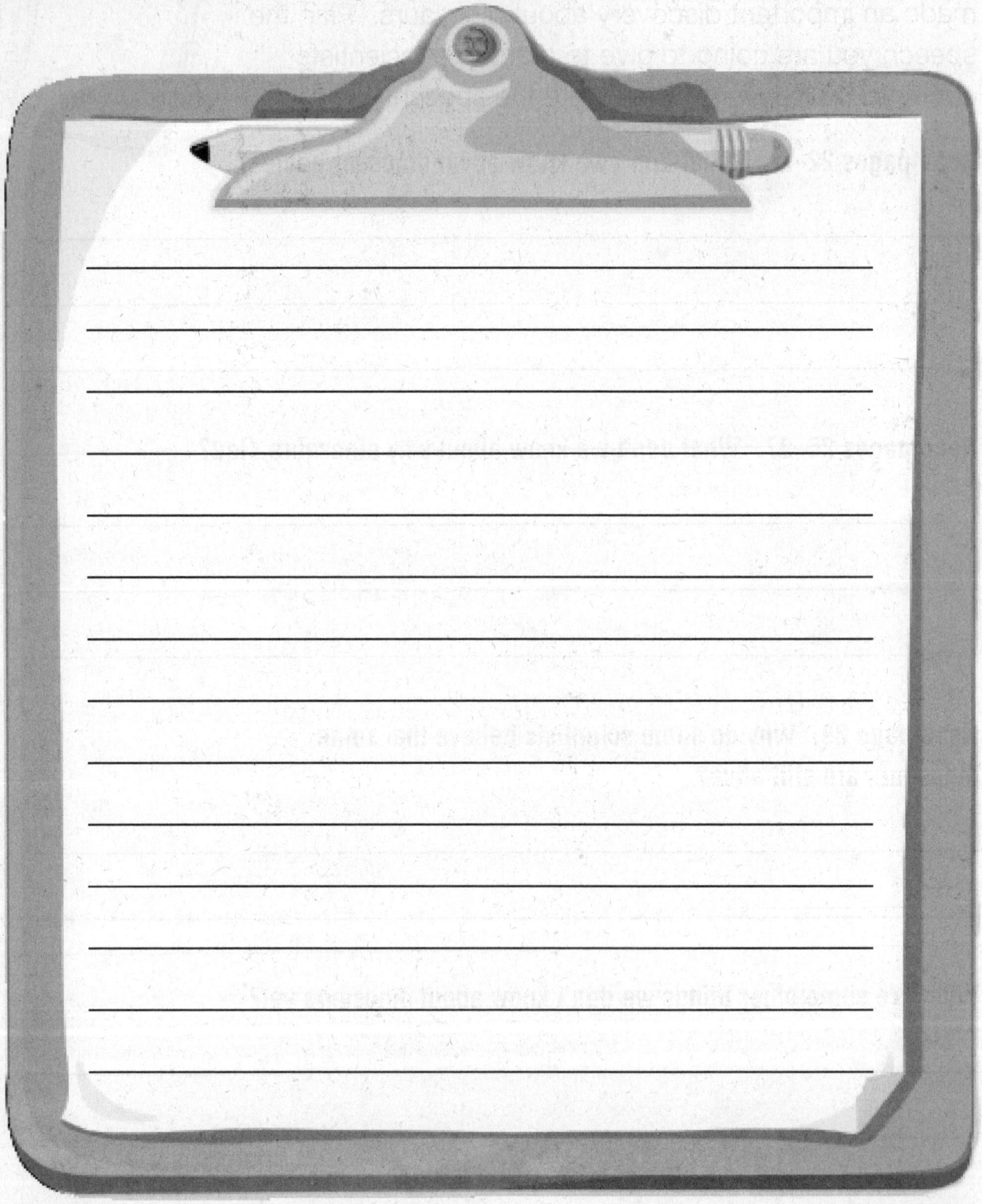

© Houghton Mifflin Harcourt Publishing Company. All rights reserved.

Name ____________________ Date ____________

Base Words and *-ed, -ing*

Read each sentence. Choose the missing word from the box. Write the word. Then reread the complete sentence.

juggling	skipped	sliced
rattled	exciting	practiced
excused	tasting	unzipped

1. Travis ____________ his jacket, took it off, and hung it up.
2. The two girls ____________ across the playground instead of walking.
3. The clown is ____________ four balls high into the air.
4. The polite man ____________ himself before he got up from the table.
5. "It was ____________ to see real giraffes at the zoo!" Keisha said.
6. Did your eyes water when you ____________ the onions?
7. When the snake ____________ its tail, we took off running.
8. I ____________ my spelling words over and over.
9. The chef is ____________ the stew to see if it needs more salt.

© Houghton Mifflin Harcourt Publishing Company. All rights reserved.

Name ______________________ Date __________

Adverbs That Compare

- **Adverbs** can tell *where, when,* or *how* something happens. Adverbs are used to describe verbs. Adverbs can also be used to compare actions.
- To compare two actions, use the ending *-er* with most adverbs, such as *hard, late,* or *slow*.
- Use *more* before adverbs that end in *-ly*, such as *carefully* or *quickly*.

She practiced harder than her brother needed to practice.
She danced more awkwardly than her brother did.

Thinking Question
Are two actions compared?

Choose the correct adverb in parentheses. Write it on the line.

1. The brother and sister acted (bashfully, more bashfully) than their father. ______________
2. Abby waited (eagerly, more eagerly) than her brother did. ______________
3. The woman sang (gently, more gently) than the wind blew. ______________
4. She swayed (gracefully, more gracefully) than the prairie grasses moved outside. ______________
5. The song sounded (stronger, more stronger) that it did before. ______________
6. The little girl held her toy bear (carefully, more carefully) than she would hold a ball. ______________

© Houghton Mifflin Harcourt Publishing Company. All rights reserved.

Name ______________________ Date ____________

Adverbs That Compare

- **Adverbs** can be used to compare two actions.
- Add *-er* to one-syllable adverbs to show comparison. If the adverb ends with *e*, drop the *e* before adding *-er*.
- Use *more* before adverbs that end in *-ly*. Sometimes, an adverb that ends with *-ly* will use an *-ier* ending.

  The moon shines brighter than the stars.

  Linda could see the moon earlier than she could notice the stars.

  The stars twinkled more brilliantly than the moon glowed.

Thinking Question
Does the adverb have more than one syllable or does it end in -ly?

Write the correct form of the adverb in parentheses to complete the sentence.

1. The truck arrived (late) today than the bus did.

   ____

2. The cornstalks stood (rigidly) than the tall grass.

   ____

3. She watched the sheep (closely) than she watched the cows. ______________
4. They climbed (high) than we could.

   ____

5. The wind is blowing (strong) now than it did this morning.

   ____

© Houghton Mifflin Harcourt Publishing Company. All rights reserved.

Name ____________________ Date __________

Spelling Word Sort

Sarah, Plain and Tall
Spelling
Words with *-ed* and *-ing*

Write each Basic Word under the correct heading.

Words with *-ed*	Words with *-ing*

Review: Add the Review Words to your Word Sort.

Challenge: Add the Challenge Words to your Word Sort.

Spelling Words

Basic

1. coming
2. swimming
3. dropping
4. tapping
5. taping
6. invited
7. saving
8. stared
9. planned
10. changing
11. joking
12. loved
13. gripped
14. tasted

Review

making
stopped

Challenge

freezing
scared

© Houghton Mifflin Harcourt Publishing Company. All rights reserved.

Name ________________________ Date ______________

Focus Trait: Ideas

Setting the Scene

Setting the scene means telling the reader who the main character or narrator is and what is happening as the story begins.

The chart below lists questions that a writer answers to set the scene. Read the example answers, and then complete the chart with answers of your own.

Questions	Example Answers	Your Answers
Who is the main character or narrator?	a young scientist	
What is he or she doing?	She is studying elephants, and she has found an injured baby elephant.	
Where and when are events taking place?	Events take place in the rain forest in Africa. It is early in the morning.	
What problem does the main character or narrator face?	The scientist must take care of the baby and bring it to an animal refuge.	

Copyright © Houghton Mifflin Company. All rights reserved.

Name ______________________ Date ____________

Cumulative Review

Read each sentence. Choose the missing word from the box. Write the word. Then reread the complete sentence.

chopped	haircut	tripped
described	included	watermelon
driveway	racing	
driving	spinning	

1. The man admired his new short ______________ in the mirror.

2. In the dark, Lee Ann ______________ and fell over a chair.

3. Martin ______________ the carrot into small pieces.

4. Mr. Ward parked his truck in the ______________.

5. The puppy is ______________ in a circle, chasing its tail!

6. A cap is ______________ as part of your baseball uniform.

7. We ate juicy ______________ at the school picnic.

8. Braden ______________ every detail of the painting.

9. It was fun to watch the two squirrels ______________ up and down the tree.

10. I saw an electric car ______________ past our school.

© Houghton Mifflin Harcourt Publishing Company. All rights reserved.

Name ______________________________ Date ________

Reader's Guide

Sarah, Plain and Tall

Write in Caleb's Diary

Help complete Caleb's diary entries with details from the story.

Read pages 209–211. How did Caleb feel before Sarah arrived?

Dear Diary,

____

____

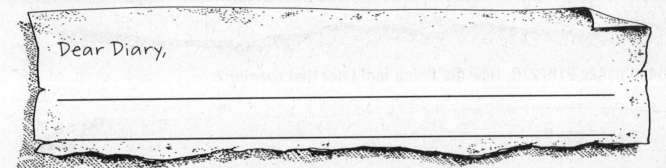

Read pages 213–215. What was it like when Caleb met Sarah?

Dear Diary,

____

____

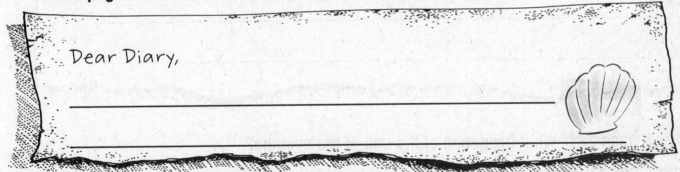

Read page 216. How did Sarah feel about living with the family? What did this make Caleb think?

Dear Diary,

____

____

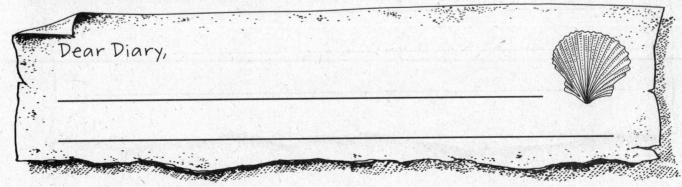

© Houghton Mifflin Harcourt Publishing Company. All rights reserved.

Read pages 217–218. How did Caleb feel when he and Anna picked flowers with Sarah?

Dear Diary,

____

____

____

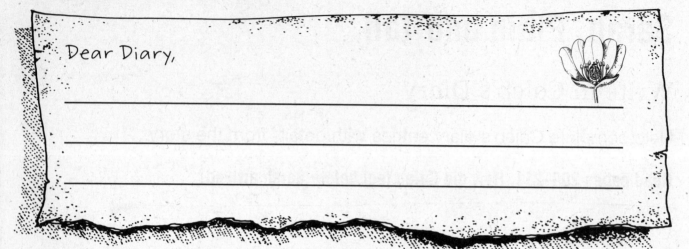

Read pages 219–220. How did Caleb feel later that evening?

Dear Diary,

____

____

____

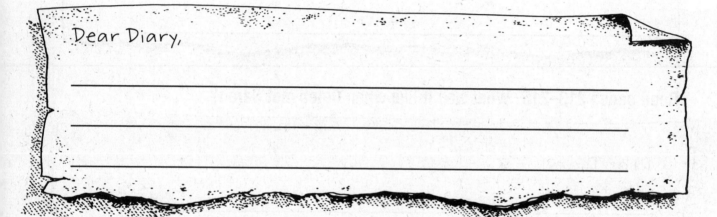

Read page 221. What happened at the end of the evening?

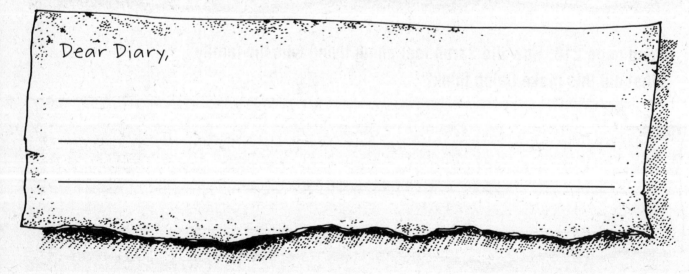

Dear Diary,

____

____

____

© Houghton Mifflin Harcourt Publishing Company. All rights reserved.

Name ____________________ Date ____________

Adverbs That Compare

Write the correct form of the adverb that compares more than two actions.

1. easily ____________________
2. furiously ____________________
3. late ____________________
4. perfectly ____________________
5. rigidly ____________________
6. high ____________________

Write the form of the adverb that compares more than two actions in parentheses.

1. Sam worked ____________________ of all the workers. (slowly)
2. Jim shoveled the ____________________ of all the adults. (quickly)
3. Sally worked the ____________________ of the three people on her team. (hard)
4. Jenny always arrived ____________________ at work. (early)

© Houghton Mifflin Harcourt Publishing Company. All rights reserved.

Name ____________________ Date __________

Words with *-ed* and *-ing*

Write the Basic Word that replaces the underlined word or words in each book title.

1. *Kidding and Laughing* ____________
2. *Moving to California* ____________
3. *Stop Letting Go of the Ball* ____________
4. *Sticking Together and Gluing Projects* ____________
5. *Moving in Water Sports* ____________
6. *Asked to the Party* ____________
7. *Pets I Have Liked a Lot* ____________
8. *Keeping Money in a Bank* ____________
9. *We Arranged a Party* ____________
10. *Making Different Weather* ____________
11. *He Held a Baseball Bat* ____________
12. *Hitting Lightly at the Door* ____________
13. *Teas I Have Tried* ____________
14. *The Monster Looked at Me!* ____________

Spelling Words

Basic

1. coming
2. swimming
3. dropping
4. tapping
5. taping
6. invited
7. saving
8. stared
9. planned
10. changing
11. joking
12. loved
13. gripped
14. tasted

Review

making
stopped

Challenge

freezing
scared

Review What Review Word completes this title?

The Art of ____________ Bread

Challenge Write your own title using one of the Challenge Words.

____

© Houghton Mifflin Harcourt Publishing Company. All rights reserved.

Name _______________ Date _______________

Prefix *non-*

Read each question. Add the prefix *non-* to the underlined word and write a new word. Use the new word to write an answer to each question.

1. A cat is a living thing. What is an example of something that is not living?

   ____

2. Violent storms, such as tornadoes, can occur on the prairie. What kind of a storm is not violent?

   ____

3. Anna and Caleb are productive when they do their chores. During the day, when are you not productive?

   ____

4. Caleb could not stop talking to Sarah. What is something you would like to do and not stop?

   ____

5. *Sarah, Plain and Tall* is fiction. What is your favorite book that is not fiction?

   ____

6. Papa, Anna, and Caleb write letters to Sarah. What is another way of communicating with someone that is not verbal?

   ____

© Houghton Mifflin Harcourt Publishing Company. All rights reserved.

Name ______________________ Date ____________

Kinds of Adjectives

Words that describe, or tell about, nouns are called **adjectives**. Adjectives can tell **what kind** or **how many** about a noun.

Jasmine loves sweet foods.

Write the adjective that tells *what kind* or *how many* about the underlined noun.

1. Tara made chocolate cake. ____________
2. Our diet has little sugar. ____________
3. We eat three kinds of vegetables. ____________
4. We drink many glasses of water daily. ____________
5. My mother makes healthful meals. ____________

Combine each pair of sentences. In the new sentence, use two adjectives to describe the same noun.

6. The vegetables are healthful. The vegetables are delicious.

____

7. The pie was sweet. It was also juicy.

____

8. The drink was thick. It was icy, too.

____

© Houghton Mifflin Harcourt Publishing Company. All rights reserved.

Name ______________________ Date ____________

Proofreading for Spelling

Read the following invitation. Find and circle the misspelled words.

You Are Invited To A Swiming Party!

Parents will be droping kids at the planed meeting place: the changging rooms at Bayview Park. Everyone is coming at 11:00.

I have been saveing plastic flowers. We will be tapeing them onto our bathing caps. People stared when we did this at my sister's party. I think they all lovved how we looked and knew we were only jokeing.

We will play in the water until noon. We griped hands at my sister's party and jumped over waves. Maybe we can do that again! Then my dad will make a tapping signal. He will serve chicken and salad for lunch. I've tastted his cooking and it will be great! Finally, we'll have a second swim. It will be a fun party. I hope you can make it!

Spelling Words

Basic

1. coming
2. swimming
3. dropping
4. tapping
5. taping
6. invited
7. saving
8. stared
9. planned
10. changing
11. joking
12. loved
13. gripped
14. tasted

Review

making
stopped

Challenge

freezing
scared

Write the misspelled words correctly on the lines below.

1. ______________ 6. ______________
2. ______________ 7. ______________
3. ______________ 8. ______________
4. ______________ 9. ______________
5. ______________ 10. ______________

© Houghton Mifflin Harcourt Publishing Company. All rights reserved.

Name _______________ Date _________

Connect to Writing

You can make your ideas clearer by using adverbs that compare. To compare two actions, add *-er* to most adverbs. Use *more* before an adverb that ends in *-ly*. To compare more than two actions, add *-est* to most adverbs. Use *most* before an adverb that ends in *-ly*.

Incorrect Adverb Form	Correct Adverb Form
Mary will arrive soonest than Ellen.	Mary will arrive sooner than Ellen.
The gray kitten acts the more lively of all the cats.	The gray kitten acts the most lively of all the cats.

Use the correct form of the adverb in parentheses. Write the sentence.

1. Ellen ran to the barn (fast) than Mary.

____

2. Mary climbed the ladder (quickly) than Ellen.

____

3. The white kitten moved (slow) of all the kittens.

____

4. The gray kitten cried (loud) than the white kitten.

____

5. Mary played with the kittens (carefully) than Ellen did.

____

© Houghton Mifflin Harcourt Publishing Company. All rights reserved.

Name ______________________ Date ____________

Spelling Changes: *-s, -es, -ed, -ing*

Read each sentence. Choose the missing word from the box. Write the word. Then reread the complete sentence.

hurried	drying	cities
replied	pennies	grazed
traveled	memories	
pillows	paintbrushes	

1. April ______________ to the question with another question.
2. I have such good ______________ of kindergarten!
3. Most of the big ______________ in California are on the coast.
4. The goats ______________ on the hillside.
5. Ten ______________ equal one dime.
6. Alexander ______________ to school so he wouldn't be late.
7. The class ______________ to the zoo on a bus.
8. Joshua broke a plate as he was ______________ the dishes.
9. Mom set two fluffy ______________ on the bed.
10. The artist had many ______________ of different sizes.

© Houghton Mifflin Harcourt Publishing Company. All rights reserved.

Name ______________________ Date ____________

Adjectives That Compare

The Journey: Stories of Migration
Grammar:
Making Comparisons

- **Adjectives** are used to describe nouns. Adjectives can also be used to **compare** two or more nouns.
- Add the ending *-er* to most adjectives to compare two nouns. Add *-est* to compare more than two nouns.

Adjective	Comparing Two Nouns	Comparing More Than Two Nouns
tall	taller	tallest
high	higher	highest
large	larger	largest

Thinking Question
How many nouns are being compared?

Kim's hair is long. Morgan's hair is longer than Kim's. Jamie's hair is the longest of all.

Write the correct form of the adjective in parentheses.

1. Monarch butterflies are (quick) than turtles.

____

2. One book showed that the butterfly was (bright) than the flower it landed on. ______________

3. The (long) section in the book was about migration.

____

4. Male monarchs are (big) than female monarchs.

____

© Houghton Mifflin Harcourt Publishing Company. All rights reserved.

Name ____________________ Date __________

Adverbs That Compare

- **Adverbs** tell *when, where,* or *how* something happened. They can also be used to **compare actions.**
- Add the ending *-er* to adverbs to compare two actions.
- To compare more than two actions, add the ending *-est.*

Adverb	Comparing Two Actions	Comparing More Than Two Actions
late	later	latest
quickly	more quickly	most quickly
fast	faster	fastest

Thinking Question
How many actions are being compared?

Len jumped high. I jumped higher than Len. Lou jumped the highest of all.

Write the correct form of the adverb in parentheses.

1. I thought the whale swam (fast) than the dolphin. ____________
2. Lee thought the dolphins swam the (fast) of all the animals we saw. ____________
3. We talked (softly) than we do in school. ____________
4. The dolphin dived (deep) than the school of fish. ____________

© Houghton Mifflin Harcourt Publishing Company. All rights reserved.

Name ______________________ Date ____________

Spelling Word Sort

Write each Basic Word under the correct heading.

Words ending with *-es*	Words ending with *-ed*

Review: Suppose you were asked to add a column for the Review Words. What would you name the heading of that column? ______________________

Challenge: **Add the Challenge Words to your Word Sort.**

Spelling Words

Basic

1. cities
2. cried
3. puppies
4. hurried
5. stories
6. flies
7. parties
8. tried
9. pennies
10. fried
11. carried
12. babies
13. spied
14. ponies

Review

pretty
very

Challenge

countries
libraries

© Houghton Mifflin Harcourt Publishing Company. All rights reserved.

Name ______________________ Date ____________

Focus Trait: Word Choice

Using Similes

Description	Simile Added
My face turned red.	My face turned as red as a tomato.

A. Read each description. Create a clearer picture by adding a simile using *like* or *as*.

Description	Simile Added
1. Huge rain clouds blocked the sun and made it dark outside.	Huge rain clouds blocked the sun and made ______________________.
2. The children walking in the hallway are loud.	The children walking in the hallway are ______ ______________________.

B. Read each description. Add a simile to each description to create a clearer picture for the reader. Write your new sentences.

Description	Simile Added
3. The freshly washed floor was slippery.	
4. The new mall is huge.	

Pair/Share **Work with a partner to brainstorm similes to add to each description.**

Copyright © Houghton Mifflin Company. All rights reserved.

Name ____________________ Date __________

Less Common Plurals

Read each sentence. Choose the missing word from the box. Write the word. Then reread each complete sentence.

knives
leaves
hooves
lives
loaves

1. The blacksmith put shoes on the horses' ______________.
2. Run for your ______________! The volcano is erupting!
3. Do you have any ______________ of wheat bread?
4. In autumn, the ______________ fall from the trees.
5. Set the table with forks, ______________, and spoons.

© Houghton Mifflin Harcourt Publishing Company. All rights reserved.

Name ______________________ Date ________

Reader's Guide

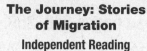

The Journey: Stories of Migration

An Interview with Locust and Whale

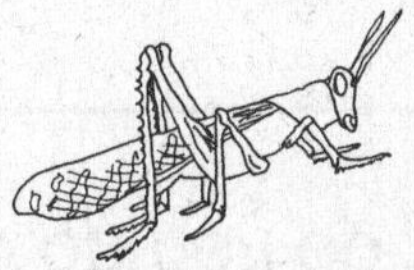

Hello and welcome to the weekly radio program, *Animal Journeys*. Today we are going to talk with Locust and Whale, two animals that take amazing journeys.

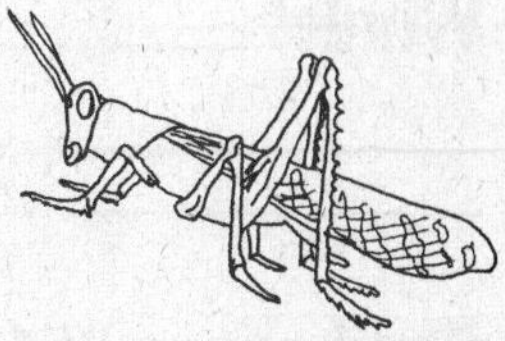

Read pages 241–242. Locust, let's hear your story first. What makes you migrate?

Locust: ______________________________

Read page 243. How interesting. What happens when you all land?

Locust: ______________________________

Read pages 246–247. Now tell us more about how you travel.

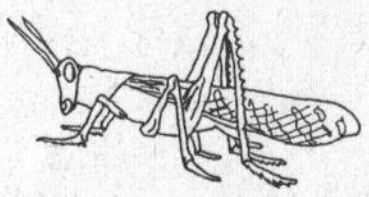

Locust: ______________________________

© Houghton Mifflin Harcourt Publishing Company. All rights reserved.

Name ______________________________ Date ______

Read pages 248–250. Whale, you migrate too but for different reasons. Why do you migrate?

Whale: ____

____

What do you do on your migration that is similar to what locusts do?

Whale: ____

____

Read pages 251–252. When you arrive at the warm tropical waters in January, what happens?

Whale: ____

____

Read pages 252–253. When spring comes, why do you migrate again?

Whale: ____

____

Thank you both for joining us on *Animal Journeys*. We have learned a lot today about your journeys across the world!

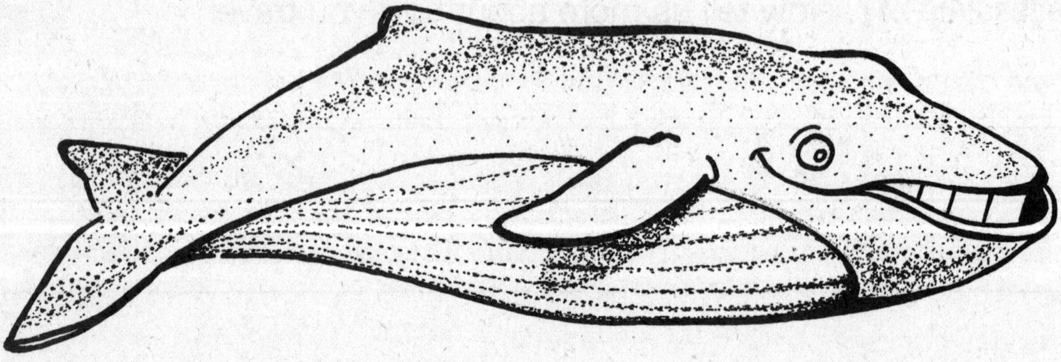

© Houghton Mifflin Harcourt Publishing Company. All rights reserved.

Name ____________________ Date ____________

Adjectives and Adverbs That Compare

Review with students that adjectives compare nouns, and adverbs compare verbs, or actions.

Write an adjective or adverb to complete each sentence. Then write *adjective* or *adverb* to identify the answer you gave.

1. A butterfly's wings move ________________ than a locust's wings. (quietly) ________________
2. Locusts are the ________________ of all insects. (hungry) ________________
3. The waves splashed ________________ than they had earlier in the day. (high) ________________
4. The waters near the Arctic are ________________ than the waters near Mexico. (cold) ________________

Write two sentences. Include an adjective that compares in one sentence and an adverb that compares in the other sentence.

5. ____

____

6. ____

____

© Houghton Mifflin Harcourt Publishing Company. All rights reserved.

Name ______________________ Date ____________

Changing Final *y* to *i*

Write the Basic Word or Words to answer each question.

1. Which word names big places? ____________
2. Which words name living things?

   ____________, ____________,

   ____________, ____________
3. Which words rhyme with lied?

   ____________, ____________,

   ____________, ____________
4. Which word names money you can carry in a pocket?

   ____
5. Which verb names what you did when you were late to something? ____________
6. What words make you think of food?

   ____________, ____________
7. Which word names things that you read?

   ____
8. Write two words that name something small.

   ____________, ____________

Review **Name a word that is an adjective.** ____________

Challenge **Write a word that names places.** ____________

Spelling Words

Basic

1. cities
2. cried
3. puppies
4. hurried
5. stories
6. flies
7. parties
8. tried
9. pennies
10. fried
11. carried
12. babies
13. spied
14. ponies

Review

pretty
very

Challenge

countries
libraries

© Houghton Mifflin Harcourt Publishing Company. All rights reserved.

Name ______________________ Date ____________

Word Roots

Read each question. Write the word root or word roots in each underlined word. Then use the underlined word to write a complete sentence to answer each question.

1. How do grasshoppers survive when there is not enough food?

____

____

2. What happens when grasshoppers transform into locusts?

____

____

3. Why are locusts so destructive to people's gardens?

____

____

4. How do locusts affect transportation?

____

____

5. When do gray whales start to look for companions?

____

____

6. What do the bodies of the gray whales demand before the whales migrate south?

____

____

© Houghton Mifflin Harcourt Publishing Company. All rights reserved.

Name ______________________ Date ____________

Adjectives and Articles

- The words *a*, *an*, and *the* are special adjectives called **articles**. Use *a* and *an* with singular nouns. Use *a* before words that begin with a consonant sound. Use *an* before words that begin with a vowel sound. Use *the* before both singular and plural nouns.
- An adjective formed from a proper noun should begin with a capital letter.

  The class took a bus to see an exhibit of African zebras.

Rewrite each sentence correctly. Capitalize proper adjectives.

1. We also saw european deer.

____

2. A irish scientist gave a talk.

____

Use proofreading marks to write *a*, *an*, and *the* correctly.

Dear Diary,

We took a trip to see butterflies. We also saw a ant as big as a spider. An guide told us about butterflies in Mexico. He described the stages of an butterfly's life. I asked him an question, and he answered it.

Ken

© Houghton Mifflin Harcourt Publishing Company. All rights reserved.

Name ______________________ Date ____________

The Journey: Stories of Migration
Spelling: Changing Final *y* to *i*

Proofreading for Spelling

Find and circle the misspelled words.

While helping Ms. Mancia in the library, I have spyed many interesting things. I made a list of some of them.

- Two pennys were found in a book about banking!
- Once a man carryed three babies in at one time. He held all three while he looked something up on the computer. Then he hurreed out.
- Two flys landed on a book titled *Insect Homes.*
- A girl cried as she looked at pictures of puppyes.
- A cookbook showed fryed chicken for Valentine's Day. Chicken on Valentine's Day?
- The title of one book was *Farm Storys from Our Big Cityes.*
- Two ponies tryd to climb in through a window. (Okay, I made that one up!)

Write the misspelled words correctly on the lines below.

1. ______________ 6. ______________
2. ______________ 7. ______________
3. ______________ 8. ______________
4. ______________ 9. ______________
5. ______________ 10. ______________

Spelling Words

Basic
1. cities
2. cried
3. puppies
4. hurried
5. stories
6. flies
7. parties
8. tried
9. pennies
10. fried
11. carried
12. babies
13. spied
14. ponies

Review
pretty
very

Challenge
countries
libraries

© Houghton Mifflin Harcourt Publishing Company. All rights reserved.

Name ______________________ Date ____________

Connect to Writing

You can make your descriptions clearer by using adjectives and adverbs that compare. To compare two nouns or actions, add *-er* to most adjectives and adverbs. To compare more than two nouns or actions, add *-est* to most adjectives and adverbs.

Adjective	Adverb
The blue fish is big.	Dad eats fast.
The white fish is bigger than the blue fish.	My sister eats faster than Dad.
The gray fish is the biggest fish in the tank.	Mom eats the fastest in the family.

Use the correct form of the adjective or adverb in parentheses. Write the sentence.

1. This aquarium is (new) than the one in Tarpon.

____

2. Tony got to the aquarium (late) than Katie.

____

3. The jellyfish tank was the (dark) tank in the aquarium.

____

4. Katie stayed at the seahorse display (long) than at the other displays.

____

____

© Houghton Mifflin Harcourt Publishing Company. All rights reserved.

Name ______________________________ Date ____________

Suffixes *-ful*, *-y*, *-ous*, *-ly*, *-er*

Read each sentence. Choose the missing word from the box. Write the word. Then reread the complete sentence.

spoonful	messy	gardener
runner	closely	windy
nervous	bravely	
graceful	joyous	

1. On a ________________ day, I have to hold onto my hat!
2. The first ________________ of soup is the hottest.
3. The ________________ dancer leaped across the stage.
4. Damian ________________ walked across the swinging bridge.
5. The ________________ planted flowers that would attract bees and butterflies.
6. The lamb followed ________________ behind its mother so it wouldn't get lost.
7. My ________________ dog spilled her food and tracked mud across the floor.
8. It was a ________________ occasion at my house when I brought home a good report card.
9. Do you feel ________________ about singing the solo in the school play?
10. When the ________________ crossed the finish line, she held her hands over her head in celebration.

© Houghton Mifflin Harcourt Publishing Company. All rights reserved.

Name ____________________ Date __________

Singular Possessive Nouns

- A **singular possessive noun** shows that a person, animal, place, or thing has or owns something.
- Add an *apostrophe* and *s* to form a singular possessive noun.

The backpack's straps were loose.
Oliver's backpack was once home to a mouse.

Thinking Question
Which noun owns or has something?

Write the possessive for each noun below.

1. friend ____________
2. Emma ____________
3. bus station ____________
4. river ____________
5. Florida ____________
6. car ____________

Underline the noun that should be possessive and write the possessive form.

7. The man hobby was to build furniture. ____________
8. The workshop tools hung neatly on the wall. ____________
9. His niece birthday was next week. ____________
10. The day chores would have to wait until he completed the gift. ____________

© Houghton Mifflin Harcourt Publishing Company. All rights reserved.

Name ____________________ Date __________

Plural Possessive Nouns

- To form a **plural possessive noun**, add an *apostrophe* to the end of plural nouns that end in *s*.
- Add an *apostrophe* and *s* to the end of plural nouns that do not end in *s*.

Raymond put the sisters' postcards in the mail.

The children's letters were from all over the country.

Thinking Question
Which noun owns or has something?

Write the possessive form of the plural nouns.

1. men ____________________
2. babies ____________________
3. books ____________________
4. fish ____________________
5. shelves ____________________

Write sentences for three of the possessive plural nouns.

6. ____
7. ____
8. ____

© Houghton Mifflin Harcourt Publishing Company. All rights reserved.

Name ______________________ Date ____________

The Journey of Oliver K. Woodman
Spelling:
The Suffixes *-ful*, *-ly*, and *-er*

Spelling Word Sort

Write each Basic Word under the correct heading.

Words that End with the Suffix *-ful*	Words that End with the Suffix *-ly*
______	______
______	______
______	______
______	______
______	______
______	______
______	______

Words that End with the Suffix *-er*	
______	______
______	______
______	______

Review: Add the Review Words to your Word Sort.

Challenge: Add the Challenge Words to your Word Sort.

Spelling Words

Basic

1. singer
2. loudly
3. joyful
4. teacher
5. fighter
6. closely
7. powerful
8. farmer
9. quickly
10. careful
11. friendly
12. speaker
13. wonderful
14. truly

Review

hopeful
safely

Challenge

listener
calmly

© Houghton Mifflin Harcourt Publishing Company. All rights reserved.

Name ______________________ Date ____________

Focus Trait: Voice

Showing Characters' Feelings

Instead of this...	*...a writer wrote this to show feelings.*
Wendy is a good friend.	Wendy is lots of fun to spend a Saturday afternoon with!

A. Read the sentence. Rewrite the sentence to show feelings.

Instead of this...	*...the author wrote this to show feelings.*
1. I liked the food.	

B. Read each event below from *The Journey of Oliver K. Woodman*. Look at the pictures on the pages listed below. Write a line of dialogue in which Oliver shows how he might have felt.

Pair/Share **Work with a partner to brainstorm words that show feelings.**

Event	Dialogue with Feelings
2. Oliver rides with three sisters. (pp. 288–289)	
3. Oliver gets to Tameka's house. (pp. 292–293)	

Copyright © Houghton Mifflin Company. All rights reserved.

Name ______________________ Date ____________

Cumulative Review

Read each sentence. Choose the missing word from the box. Write the word. Then reread the complete sentence.

salty	handful	numerous
juicy	baker	happily
beautiful	butcher	
finely	dangerous	

1. There are ______________ kinds of snacks, and there are many healthful ones to choose from.
2. A ______________ of raisins is a good snack. You can grab them and go!
3. Some people like ______________ snacks like pretzels or nuts.
4. A ______________ can make muffins and breads.
5. Not only do bakeries smell good but the items are ______________ to look at.
6. ______________ sliced cheese goes well with crackers.
7. There is nothing like a ______________ orange as a snack. You can eat it or squeeze it into a glass and drink it.
8. A knife is a ______________ tool. The sharp edge could cut a child's fingers.
9. A ______________ is trained in using very sharp knives to cut meat.
10. After your snack, smile and go ______________ on with your day!

Copyright © Houghton Mifflin Company. All rights reserved.

Name ____________________ Date ________

Reader's Guide

The Journey of Oliver K. Woodman

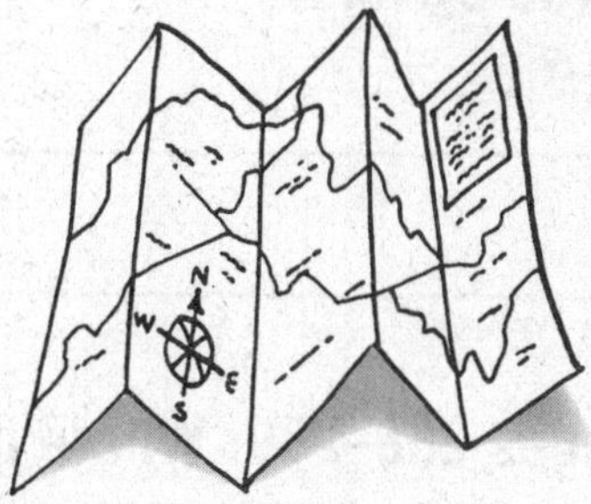

A Timeline of Oliver's Journey

Oliver K. Woodman spent two months traveling from Uncle Ray's house to Tameka's house. First, use details from the text and illustrations to gather information. Then show Oliver's journey on a timeline.

Read pages 274–278. According to Uncle Ray's second letter, when did Oliver K. Woodman begin his journey? Where did he start?

____

____

Read pages 279–280. When did Uncle Ray get news of Oliver again? Where was he?

____

Read page 281. When did Uncle Ray next hear about Oliver? Where was Oliver at that time?

____

____

Read page 282. When did Uncle Ray get news next? Where was Oliver?

____

____

© Houghton Mifflin Harcourt Publishing Company. All rights reserved.

Name ______________________________ Date ______

Read pages 286–287. Uncle Ray and Tameka thought Oliver was lost. When did Uncle Ray get news from Oliver? Where was Oliver?

____

____

Read pages 288–289. Where did Oliver end up next? When?

____

____

Now use the details that you have gathered to complete the timeline below. Remember to use all the dates from the letters to Uncle Ray that told when Oliver was in each place.

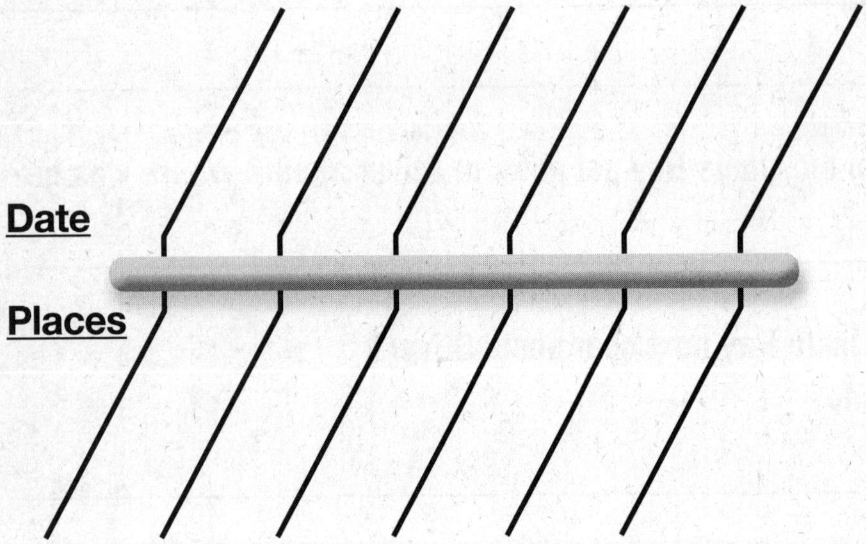

© Houghton Mifflin Harcourt Publishing Company. All rights reserved.

Name ______________________ Date ____________

Possessive Pronouns

The Journey of Oliver K. Woodman
Grammar: Possessive Nouns and Pronouns

Read the sentences below. Underline the possessive pronouns. If the possessive pronoun is not written correctly, write the word correctly on the line.

1. Lucy, a friend of our's, is traveling with us to Tennessee.

   ____

2. Is this his's map?

   ____

3. My favorite part of a road trip is the snacks.

   ____

4. That is hers backpack.

   ____

5. Is this yours sandwich?

   ____

Write a sentence for each of the possessive pronouns.

6. their

   ____

7. our

   ____

8. my

   ____

© Houghton Mifflin Harcourt Publishing Company. All rights reserved.

Name ______________________ Date ____________

The Suffixes *-ful, -ly,* and *-er*

Write a Basic Word to complete each sentence.

1. A person singing in a choir is a ______________.
2. If your friends yell during a game, they are playing ______________.
3. A person who grows corn in the country is a ______________.
4. If you run fast, you are moving ______________.
5. If you are very happy, you are ______________.
6. The person whose desk is in the front of your classroom is your ______________.
7. Someone who is very strong is ______________.
8. When you use scissors, you should be ______________.
9. A person who smiles and asks you how you are feeling is ______________.
10. If you are ______________ sorry, you will make a sincere apology.

Spelling Words

Basic

1. singer
2. loudly
3. joyful
4. teacher
5. fighter
6. closely
7. powerful
8. farmer
9. quickly
10. careful
11. friendly
12. speaker
13. wonderful
14. truly

Review

hopeful
safely

Challenge

listener
calmly

Review: Choose a Review Word that completes the sentence.

If you want something to happen, you are ______________.

Challenge: Choose a Challenge Word. Use it in a sentence.

____

© Houghton Mifflin Harcourt Publishing Company. All rights reserved.

Name ______________________ Date __________

Suffixes *-er*, *-est*

Read the paragraph. Circle the words with the suffix *-er* or *-est*. Then write the words the suffixes were added to on the lines below.

Saturday was the loveliest, sunniest day we have had during our car trip. The weather in San Francisco was colder than I had expected, though. We walked across the Golden Gate Bridge and met the kindest people. They were nice to take photos of us. Leaving San Francisco was harder than leaving Salt Lake City had been, but we were all happier when we thought about our next adventure.

1. ______________	4. ______________
2. ______________	5. ______________
3. ______________	6. ______________

Add the suffix *-er* or *-est* to create new words. Complete the sentence.

7. **nice:** Raymond Johnson is the ______________ uncle in the world!

8. **dark:** The sky is ______________ tonight than it was last night.

9. **strange:** This is the ______________ trip I have ever taken!

10. **young:** My sister, Lucinda, is two years ______________ than I am.

© Houghton Mifflin Harcourt Publishing Company. All rights reserved.

Name ______________________ Date ____________

The Special Verb *be*

- The verbs *am*, *is*, *are*, *was*, and *were* are forms of the verb *be*. They do not show action. They tell what someone or something is or was. *Am*, *is*, and *are* show present tense. *Was* and *were* show past tense.

  The trip <u>is</u> fun. The trip <u>was</u> fun.

Write the verb. Write *present* or *past* for each verb.

1. The boys are tired of traveling. ______________________
2. We were away for one week. ______________________
3. I am ready to go on another trip. ______________________

Combine two short sentences by moving one predicate to make one longer sentence with two predicates. Write the new sentence on the line.

4. Father is a good driver. Father is tired of driving.

   ____

5. We are out of the car. We are ready to relax.

   ____

6. Mother and Jorge are happy. Mother and Jorge are in the house.

   ____

© Houghton Mifflin Harcourt Publishing Company. All rights reserved.

Name ____________________ Date __________

Proofreading for Spelling

The Journey of Oliver K. Woodman
Spelling:
The Suffixes *-ful*, *-ly*, and *-er*

Read the following letter. Circle the misspelled words.

Dear Marcus,

My class heard a speeker today. His name was Mr. Brown. He showed us pictures of different parts of the country. We saw a picture of a farmar on his farm. I looked at the picture closelie to see all the animals.

We saw pictures of the Rocky Mountains. What a wunderful trip that would be! I am hopefull that someday I will see the mountains.

Some of my friends were talking lowdley. Mrs. Garcia told them to be quiet. Mrs. Garcia is our teachur.

Mr. Brown answered all of our questions. He was very frenly.

After the speech, we all went kuikly back to our classrooms. I was carefull not to bump into anyone on the way.

Your friend,
Danny

Spelling Words

Basic

1. singer
2. loudly
3. joyful
4. teacher
5. fighter
6. closely
7. powerful
8. farmer
9. quickly
10. careful
11. friendly
12. speaker
13. wonderful
14. truly

Review

hopeful
safely

Challenge

listener
calmly

Write the misspelled words correctly on the lines below.

1. ____________ 6. ____________
2. ____________ 7. ____________
3. ____________ 8. ____________
4. ____________ 9. ____________
5. ____________ 10. ____________

© Houghton Mifflin Harcourt Publishing Company. All rights reserved.

Name ______________________ Date ____________

Connect to Writing

You can make your sentences smoother by replacing repeated possessive nouns with possessive pronouns. Make sure the possessive pronoun matches the possessive noun you replace.

Awkward Sentence	Smoother Sentence
My brother's favorite toy is my brother's wooden car.	My brother's favorite toy is his wooden car.
"My cousins' friends are going to my cousins' house," she said.	"My cousins' friends are going to their house," she said.

Replace the underlined possessive noun with a possessive pronoun. Write the sentence.

1. Lucy's favorite aunt is <u>Lucy's</u> Aunt Debra.

   ____

2. The family's first stop will be at the <u>family's</u> old house.

   ____

3. Jack let Lucy borrow <u>Jack's</u> headphones for the trip.

   ____

4. "Will Aunt Debra's new puppy be at <u>Aunt Debra's</u> house?" Lucy asked.

   ____

5. Dad said, "Hand me <u>Dad's</u> car keys."

   ____

© Houghton Mifflin Harcourt Publishing Company. All rights reserved.

Name _______________ Date _________

Dog-of-the-Sea-Waves
Phonics: Prefixes *un-, pre-, re-, bi-*

Prefixes *un-*, *pre-*, *re-*, *bi-*

Read each sentence. Choose the missing word from the box. Write the word. Then reread the complete sentence.

refilled	preview	unsafe	unbroken
preheat	unopened	biweekly	bicycle
redo	pretest		

1. Did you see the old _______________ zoom past?
2. It is _______________ to skateboard without a helmet.
3. The _______________ showed parts of a new movie.
4. I have to study the words I missed on the spelling _______________.
5. The _______________ magazine comes out every two weeks.
6. Mom _______________ my glass after I finished the first glass of juice.
7. I was happy to find the vase _______________ after I saw it fall.
8. Tomas had to _______________ the poster after he misspelled a word on it.
9. I left the gifts _______________ while I waited for my sisters to come home.
10. The recipe says to _______________ the oven to 325 degrees before putting the chicken in.

© Houghton Mifflin Harcourt Publishing Company. All rights reserved.

Name ____________________ Date __________

Complex Sentences

- An **independent clause** is a simple sentence and tells a complete thought. It has a subject and a verb.
- A **dependent clause** has a subject and a verb, but it does not tell a complete thought.
- A **complex sentence** is formed by combining one independent clause and one or more dependent clauses.

Although the boat needed a repair. We went sailing.

Although the boat needed a repair, we went sailing.

Thinking Question
Which part of the sentence tells a complete thought? Which part cannot stand alone?

Write *complex* if the sentence has an independent clause and one or more dependent clauses. Write *dependent clause* if the sentence does not tell a complete thought.

1. When the boat's rope broke, the boys worked quickly to fix it.

   ____

2. Jen retied the ropes since she was good with knots.

   ____

3. While the captain carefully watched her.

   ____

4. Everyone relaxed when they arrived at the dock.

   ____

© Houghton Mifflin Harcourt Publishing Company. All rights reserved.

Name ____________________ Date ____________

Subordinating Conjunctions

- A complex sentence is formed by combining one independent clause and at least one dependent clause. If the dependent clause appears first, add a comma after it.
- **Subordinating conjunctions** begin dependent clauses. Some subordinating conjunctions are *after, although, because, before, even though, since, unless, until, when, while.*

We had fun swimming. Because of the weather.

We had fun swimming because of the weather.

Thinking Question
Which subordinating conjunction can join the dependent clause to the independent clause?

Underline the dependent clause. Write the subordinating conjunction that begins the dependent clause.

1. We will see the dolphins before we leave.

____

2. After we eat lunch we will see more of the zoo.

____

3. Because he forgot his lunch we went back to the car.

____

4. We will miss the dolphins unless we hurry.

____

© Houghton Mifflin Harcourt Publishing Company. All rights reserved.

Name ______________________ Date __________

Spelling Word Sort

Dog-of-the-Sea-Waves
Spelling:
The Prefixes *re-* and *un-*

Write each Basic Word under the correct heading.

Prefix that means "again"	Prefix that means "not" or "opposite of"

Review: Add the Review Words to your Word Sort.

Challenge: Add the Challenge Words to your Word Sort.

Spelling Words

Basic

1. unfold
2. rejoin
3. untie
4. reheat
5. unfair
6. unclear
7. repaid
8. rewrite
9. unhurt
10. recheck
11. unlucky
12. unwrap
13. reuse
14. unsure

Review

reread
unsafe

Challenge

unbuckle
unknown

© Houghton Mifflin Harcourt Publishing Company. All rights reserved.

Name ______________________ Date ____________

Focus Trait: Ideas
Using Vivid Details

Good story writers use vivid details to paint a clear picture. Compare the sentence without vivid details to the one with vivid details.

Without Vivid Details: The beach was beautiful in the morning.

With Vivid Details: The sunrise cast a warm glow over the golden sands of the empty beach.

Rewrite each sentence, adding vivid details. You may use ideas from the box below or think of your own.

gently	sparkling	shady	cool

1. They had to cross the ocean to get home.

____

2. Manu cleaned the animal's wound.

____

3. He built a shelter from the sun.

____

4. He gathered berries.

____

5. He dived into the water.

____

© Houghton Mifflin Harcourt Publishing Company. All rights reserved.

Name ______________________ Date __________

Cumulative Review

Read each sentence. Choose the missing word from the box. Write the word.

bimonthly	revisit	unequal	rebuild
reelected	preheat	unfriendly	unknown

1. I had so much fun at the park that I hope we ______________ it next summer.

2. I asked Uncle Ramon to pour more water into my glass because the amounts in the two glasses were ______________.

3. Be sure to ______________ the oven before you put the biscuits in to bake.

4. The mayor was ______________ for a second term after all the votes were counted.

5. The ______________ school newspaper comes out on the first and fifteenth of the month.

6. The ______________ store clerk did not look up when I said hello.

7. There was no card on the flowers that were sent by an ______________ person.

8. The carpenter had to ______________ the wobbly bookshelves.

© Houghton Mifflin Harcourt Publishing Company. All rights reserved.

Name ______________________ Date ______

Reader's Guide

Dog-of-the-Sea-Waves

Homes for Sale!

When the brothers returned home to the southern sea, they wanted to convince other people to move there. They decided to place an advertisement in the newspaper.

Read page 315. What are some details on this page that will convince people to move to the Hawaiian Islands?

____

____

____

____

Read pages 318–319. Here, Manu finds the hurt seal. How can the story of the seal help convince people to move to the islands?

____

____

Read pages 320–321. On these pages, the brothers were gathering food. What kinds of food did they gather? Do you think these details can help convince other people that Hawaii is a good place to live?

____

____

© Houghton Mifflin Harcourt Publishing Company. All rights reserved.

Name ______________________ Date ________

Now make the advertisement! Show why Hawaii will be a good place to live. The illustration should show the thing you think people would like best about Hawaii. Label the illustration and use details you gathered to write a caption about Hawaii.

© Houghton Mifflin Harcourt Publishing Company. All rights reserved.

Name ______________________ Date ____________

Forming Complex Sentences

Combine the clauses to form complex sentences.

1. Even though he is a dog. Rover is Lucy's best friend.

____

2. She takes Rover to the park. After she comes home from school.

____

3. Lucy worried she would be late. Unless she hurried.

____

4. They stayed at the park. Until it started to rain.

____

5. Because it was raining. They ran to the house.

____

6. When they got home. Rover shook water everywhere.

____

© Houghton Mifflin Harcourt Publishing Company. All rights reserved.

Name ______________________ Date ____________

Prefixes *re-*, *-un*

Write a Basic Word to answer each clue.

1. You might do this with shoe laces. ____________
2. You would do this to a present wrapped in paper.
   ____
3. You might feel this way if you didn't know the answer to a question. ____________
4. To be sure your answers on a test were correct, you might do this. ____________
5. If you thought someone had cheated in a game, you might think the game was this. ____________
6. You could do this to make some leftover food warm again. ____________
7. If you didn't like a poem you had written, you might do this to it. ____________
8. You would do this to a shirt you found folded in a drawer. ____________

Review: Choose a Review Word. Write a clue for it.

____

Challenge: Choose a Challenge Word. Write a clue for it.

____

Spelling Words

Basic

1. unfold
2. rejoin
3. untie
4. reheat
5. unfair
6. unclear
7. repaid
8. rewrite
9. unhurt
10. recheck
11. unlucky
12. unwrap
13. reuse
14. unsure

Review

reread
unsafe

Challenge

unbuckle
unknown

© Houghton Mifflin Harcourt Publishing Company. All rights reserved.

Name ______________________ Date ____________

Shades of Meaning

Read each sentence. Choose the word from the box that best completes each sentence. Explain your choice.

knows	suspects	wonders	believes	hears
know	suspect	wonder	believe	hear

1. How does Hoku ______________ that the star he discovered always points north?

   ____

   ____

2. As the brothers sail away from the island, Opua ______________ whether he sees smoke or a cloud.

   ____

   ____

3. For a while, the brothers ______________ that Manu has drowned in the sea.

   ____

   ____

4. Although they are leaving the island, Manu ______________ that he and his brothers will return.

   ____

   ____

© Houghton Mifflin Harcourt Publishing Company. All rights reserved.

Name ______________________ Date __________

Possessive Nouns and Pronouns

- A possessive noun shows that a person, place, or thing has or owns something.
- Add an apostrophe and *s* to a singular noun to make it possessive. Add an apostrophe to a plural noun that ends in *s*.
- Possessive pronouns can take the place of possessive nouns. Possessive pronouns show ownership: *my, your, his, her, its, our, their.*

The family's outing was to the zoo.
The seals' pool was new.
Their bodies moved quickly through the water.

Use the correct possessive form of the noun in parentheses to complete each sentence.

1. It was ______________ first visit to the zoo. (Charlie)
2. The ______________ Australia section has koalas. (zoo)
3. The ______________ uniforms are a dark green. (workers)

Use a possessive pronoun to take the place of the underlined possessive noun. Write the sentence.

4. Yolanda saw the dolphin's head peek out of the water.

____

5. The dolphin splashed water onto Yolanda's shoes.

____

© Houghton Mifflin Harcourt Publishing Company. All rights reserved.

Name ______________________ Date ____________

Proofreading for Spelling

Dog-of-the-Sea-Waves
Spelling:
Prefixes *re-*, *-un*

Read each direction. Circle the misspelled words.

1. Set up your tent. First, unfolde the tent.

2. Next, unrap the tent ropes. You need the ropes to set up your tent.

3. If ropes are tied, you need to untye them.

4. Try to reus plastic bags while at camp. Do not throw them away.

5. Do not reheet drinks or food. See your camp leader.

6. Be sure to rejoyn your group after lunch.

7. Always walk with a friend. Walking alone at camp is unsaff.

8. Are you sure you have everything? You should rechek your bag.

Spelling Words

1. unfold
2. rejoin
3. untie
4. reheat
5. unfair
6. unclear
7. repaid
8. rewrite
9. unhurt
10. recheck
11. unlucky
12. unwrap
13. reuse
14. unsure

Review
reread
unsafe

Challenge
unbuckle
unknown

Write the misspelled words correctly on the lines below.

1. ______________ 5. ______________

2. ______________ 6. ______________

3. ______________ 7. ______________

4. ______________ 8. ______________

© Houghton Mifflin Harcourt Publishing Company. All rights reserved.

Name ______________________ Date ____________

Connect to Writing

Short, choppy sentences can be combined to make your writing smoother. Use a subordinating conjunction to form complex sentences. Remember to use a comma after the dependent clause if it comes first in the sentence.

Short Sentences	Longer, Smoother Sentences
Sam taught his cat. He thought the cat was clever.	Sam taught his cat since he thought the cat was clever.
Dave played with his pet. He was happy.	While Dave played with his pet, he was happy.

Use a subordinating conjunction from the word bank to combine two short, choppy sentences. Write the new sentence on the line.

Word Bank

since while though because

1. Tara's dog swims with her. It is not fond of water.

____

2. Ernesto worked with his bird. He waited for his friend.

____

3. His bird escapes often. It knows how to open its cage.

____

4. Bennie's cat is still healing. It needs to wear a bandage.

____

© Houghton Mifflin Harcourt Publishing Company. All rights reserved.

Name ______________________ Date ____________

Suffixes *-less*, *-ness*, *-able*

Mountains: Surviving on Mt. Everest
Phonics:
Suffixes *-less*, *-ness*, *-able*

Read each sentence. Choose the missing word from the box. Write the word. Then reread the complete sentence.

boneless	predictable	enjoyable	happiness
painless	weightless	shyness	softness
breakable	darkness		

1. Patricia got over her ______________ when she met the new neighors' puppy.

2. That story was so ______________ that I guessed the ending.

3. The newborn chicks are so light that they almost feel ______________.

4. I needed a flashlight to see in the ______________.

5. Since I didn't need a shot, my doctor's visit was ______________.

6. Chris smiled and clapped at the end of the ______________ movie.

7. Be careful not to drop the box because it contains ______________ items.

8. Mr. Griffin said, "The children in my classroom have brought me much joy and ______________."

9. When you eat ______________ chicken there are no bones left on the plate!

10. Bradley sank back into the ______________ of the pillow.

© Houghton Mifflin Harcourt Publishing Company. All rights reserved.

Name ______________________ Date ____________

Adjectives That Compare

- Use *-er* and *more* to compare two nouns. Use *-est* and *most* to compare three or more nouns.
- Add *-er* or *-est* to most **adjectives** that have one syllable.
- For adjectives that have two syllables and end in *-y*, such as *happy*, replace the *y* with *i* and then add *-er* or *-est*.
- Add *more* or *most* before adjectives that have three or more syllables.

Thinking Question
How many does the adjective compare? Does it have more than two syllables? Does it end in -y?

Write the correct form of the adjective in parentheses. Then write *two* or *three or more* to explain the form you wrote.

1. This backpack is (light) than that one. ____________
2. I think that mountain climbing is (dangerous) than hiking trails. ____________
3. The winds on this mountain are the (powerful) I have ever experienced. ____________
4. The trail going up was (uneven) than the trail coming down. ____________
5. Our pack mule was the (noisy) animal on the trail. ____________

© Houghton Mifflin Harcourt Publishing Company. All rights reserved.

Name ______________________ Date ____________

Adverbs That Compare

- Use *-er* or *more* to compare two verbs, or actions. Use *-est* or *most* to compare three or more.
- Add *-er* or *-est* to most **adverbs** that have one syllable.
- Add *more* or *most* before adverbs that end in *-ly*.

  Caroline climbed <u>more carefully</u> than Elena.
  Jena climbed the <u>most carefully</u>.
  Elena climbed <u>higher</u> then Jena.
  Caroline climbed the <u>highest</u>.

Thinking Question
How many does the adverb compare? Does it end in -ly?

Write the correct form of the adverb in parentheses. Then write *two* or *three or more* to explain the form you wrote.

1. Will waited (patiently) than Kyle for the storm to pass.

____

2. Kyle handled the ropes for the tent (roughly) of all the climbers.

____

3. The ropes were tied (tight) by the oldest climber.

____

4. The climbers sitting by the fire felt (warm) than those inside the tent.

____

5. Will slept (quietly) of all the campers.

____

© Houghton Mifflin Harcourt Publishing Company. All rights reserved.

Name ______________________ Date ____________

Spelling Word Sort

Mountains: Surviving on Mt. Everest
Spelling:
The Suffixes *-less* and *-ness*

Write each Basic Word under the correct heading.

Suffix that means "without"	Suffix that means "quality of being"

Challenge: **Add the Challenge Words to your Word Sort.**

Spelling Words

Basic

1. painless
2. sickness
3. sadness
4. helpless
5. thankless
6. kindness
7. hopeless
8. darkness
9. fearless
10. thickness
11. careless
12. goodness
13. spotless
14. softness

Review

useful
weakly

Challenge

breathless
eagerness

© Houghton Mifflin Harcourt Publishing Company. All rights reserved.

Name ____________________ Date __________

Mountains: Surviving on Mt. Everest
Writing:
Narrative Writing

Focus Trait: Word Choice

Choosing Words for Effect

Without strong words: Very cold winds blew hard.
With strong words for effect: Icy winds **roared by**.

Rewrite each sentence. Choose a stronger word or phrase from the box to replace the underlined word or phrase.

plunged	After nightfall	towering	terrible
fought	crush	summit	be wary of

1. Mt. Everest is a very tall mountain.

____

2. Temba made a bad mistake and took off his gloves.

____

3. When it was dark, the temperature went way down.

____

4. Temba worked hard to reach the top.

____

5. Climbers must watch out for huge pieces of ice that could fall on them.

____

Copyright © Houghton Mifflin Company. All rights reserved.

Name ____________________ Date __________

Cumulative Review

Read each sentence. Choose the missing word from the box. Write the word. Then reread the complete sentence.

redo	sleepless	freshness	crispness
preview	erasable	tasteless	valuable

1. Justin spent a ____________ night at the campout because he was worried about bears.
2. To test the ____________ of celery, see if it makes a snapping sound.
3. The painting is ____________ because it is one of a kind.
4. After one sip of the ____________ soup, Tessa switched and ate something with more flavor.
5. I like to draw in pencil because it is ____________, and I can fix my mistakes.
6. Daniel always smells each melon to test its ____________ before buying it.
7. I made so many mistakes, I had to ____________ the whole assignment.
8. We got to ____________ the movie before it came to the local theater.

© Houghton Mifflin Harcourt Publishing Company. All rights reserved.

Reader's Guide

Mountains: Surviving on Mt. Everest

Create a Travel Brochure

You are writing a travel brochure about climbing Mount Everest. First, gather details for the brochure.

Read pages 349 and 351. Write important details about Mount Everest and its mountain range.

____

____

____

Read page 354. What equipment should travelers bring?

____

____

____

Read pages 355 and 360. What should travelers know about the climb? What should they be careful *not* to do?

____

____

____

© Houghton Mifflin Harcourt Publishing Company. All rights reserved.

Name ______________________ Date ______

Now use all the details from the previous page to write a brochure that will tell climbers what to expect on Mount Everest and what to bring for the climb. Include a title and labeled illustrations on each panel of the brochure to show what that section talks about.

Preparing to Climb Mount Everest.

© Houghton Mifflin Harcourt Publishing Company. All rights reserved.

Name ______________________ Date ____________

Adjectives and Adverbs That Compare

Write an adjective or adverb to complete each sentence. Then write *adjective* or *adverb* to tell about the word or phrase you used.

1. Jeff explained the day's events ______________ than Ella. (calm) ______________
2. The water at the bottom of the stream was ______________ than the water on the surface. (murky) ______________
3. Laurie was the ______________ worker of them all. (fast) ______________
4. Jason had the ______________ sneakers in the group. (muddy) ______________

Write two sentences. Include an adjective that compares in one sentence and an adverb that compares in the other sentence.

5. ____

____

6. ____

____

© Houghton Mifflin Harcourt Publishing Company. All rights reserved.

Name ______________________ Date __________

The Suffixes -*less* and -*ness*

Write the Basic Word that makes sense in the sentence.

1. The hiker thanked the guide for her help and ______________.

2. In high mountains, a lack of oxygen can cause ______________.

3. Being ______________ in the mountains is dangerous.

4. It is not wise to climb mountains in ______________.

5. The ______________ guide climbed the high cliff.

6. I was amazed at the ______________ of the freshly fallen snow.

7. Scientists measured the ______________ of the ice at the top.

Challenge: **Choose a Challenge Word. Use it in a sentence.**

____

____

Spelling Words

Basic

1. painless
2. sickness
3. sadness
4. helpless
5. thankless
6. kindness
7. hopeless
8. darkness
9. fearless
10. thickness
11. careless
12. goodness
13. spotless
14. softness

Review

useful
weakly

Challenge

breathless
eagerness

© Houghton Mifflin Harcourt Publishing Company. All rights reserved.

Name ____________________ Date ____________

Analogies

Complete the analogies with a word from the box.

danger	increase	assist	departure
succeed	brave	slope	strength

1. Believable is to unbelievable as weakness is to ____________.
2. Force is to power as achieve is to ____________.
3. Polite is to rude as fearful is to ____________.
4. Excellent is to wonderful as risk is to ____________.
5. Frequent is to often as aid is to ____________
6. Up is to down as arrival is to ____________
7. Sad is to happy as decrease is to ____________
8. Ocean is to wave as mountain is to ____________

© Houghton Mifflin Harcourt Publishing Company. All rights reserved.

Name ______________________ Date __________

Forming Complex Sentences

- A **complex sentence** is formed by combining one independent clause and one or more dependent clauses. If the dependent clause appears first, add a comma after it.
- **Subordinating conjunctions** begin dependent clauses. Some subordinating clauses are: *after, although, because, before, even though, since, unless, until, when, while.*

Combine the clauses to form complex sentences.

1. Even though he was tired. Tracy hiked up the hill.

   ____

2. Torry planned to climb the hill. When her father could join her.

   ____

3. Because she is afraid of heights. Rita will not climb.

   ____

4. Until he saw the hill. Robbie was eager to climb.

   ____

5. They played catch. While they waited for the others to climb.

   ____

6. Mel climbed again. Before they went home.

   ____

© Houghton Mifflin Harcourt Publishing Company. All rights reserved.

Name ______________________ Date ____________

Proofreading for Spelling

Mountains: Surviving on Mt. Everest
Spelling:
The Suffixes -*less* and -*ness*

Read each journal entry. Circle the misspelled words.

Journal of a Mountain Guide

Monday: We rescued a hiker who had become lost in the darkniss.

Tuesday: It is hopless to teach some people how to be careful in the mountains. They just don't pay attention.

Wednesday: We took a short hike to the ranger station. It was paneless.

Thursday: Felt a strange thikness in my leg. I'll have a doctor check it tomorrow. Was glad for the softnes of my sleeping bag.

Friday: Found a hammer and some rope in the snow. Some careluss hiker must have dropped them.

Saturday: Some hikers thanked us for our kineness. I guess being a mountain guide is not always a thankliss job!

Spelling Words

Basic
1. painless
2. sickness
3. sadness
4. helpless
5. thankless
6. kindness
7. hopeless
8. darkness
9. fearless
10. thickness
11. careless
12. goodness
13. spotless
14. softness

Review
useful
weakly

Challenge
breathless
eagerness

Write the misspelled words correctly on the lines below.

1. ______________ 5. ______________

2. ______________ 6. ______________

3. ______________ 7. ______________

4. ______________ 8. ______________

© Houghton Mifflin Harcourt Publishing Company. All rights reserved.

Name ______________________ Date ____________

Mountains: Surviving on Mt. Everest
Grammar: Connect to Writing

Connect to Writing

Use adjectives and adverbs that compare to make your ideas easier for readers to picture. To compare two nouns or actions, add *-er* to most adjectives and adverbs. To compare more than two nouns or actions, add *-est* to most adjectives and adverbs. Use *more* or *most* before an adverb that ends in *-ly*.

	Compare Two	Compare More Than Two
Adjective	Molly's backpack is heavier than Jeff's.	Steven has the heaviest backpack of everyone in the class.
Adverb	Stacy climbs more easily than Brett.	Mike climbs most easily of everyone in the group.

Choose the correct form of the adjective or adverb in parentheses. Write the sentence.

1. Mrs. Brown's map is (newer, newest) than my map.

____

2. Where are the (higher, highest) mountains in the world?

____

3. Brynn spoke (more eagerly, most eagerly) about climbing than Jo.

____

4. Of all the climbers, Lucas climbed (more powerfully, most powerfully).

____

© Houghton Mifflin Harcourt Publishing Company. All rights reserved.

Name ______________________ Date ____________

The Foot Race Across America
Phonics: Common Final Syllables *-tion, -sion, -ture*

Common Final Syllables

Choose a word from the box to complete each sentence. Read the completed sentence.

Word Bank				
action	attention	confusion	discussion	furniture
future	motion	nature	picture	protection

1. Give me the camera and I will take your ________________.

2. No one knew what to do, so there was a lot of ________________.

3. If you push the toy car, you set it in ________________.

4. This is important news, so pay ________________.

5. Yesterday is the past, and tomorrow is the ________________.

6. An umbrella gives you ________________ from the rain.

7. Let's have a ________________ to talk about our plans.

8. Tables, chairs, and sofas are kinds of ________________.

9. I like that pirate movie because it has lots of ________________.

10. Trees, animals, and clouds are all parts of ________________.

© Houghton Mifflin Harcourt Publishing Company. All rights reserved.

Name ______________________ Date ______

Reader's Guide

The Foot Race Across America

Write a Speech

Andy Payne is receiving an award after the race, but first he must give a speech. Note important details from the text before you write the speech.

Read page 7. What were the specific details of the race that Andy saw in the newspaper?

____

____

Why did Andy want to run in the race?

____

____

Read pages 8–9. What was the first part of the race like?

____

____

Read page 10. What troubles did Andy and the runners face?

____

____

Read pages 12–14. What happened at the end of the race?

____

____

© Houghton Mifflin Harcourt Publishing Company. All rights reserved.

Name ______________________ Date ________

The announcer steps onto the stage and says, "We will now present the award for Greatest Running Achievement to Andy Payne. Andy, please tell us about the race!" Write Andy's speech.

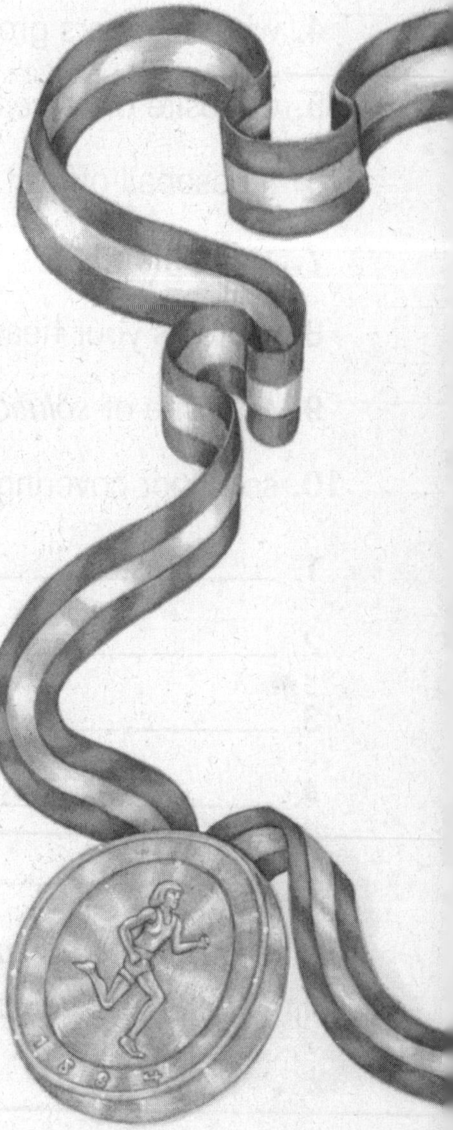

© Houghton Mifflin Harcourt Publishing Company. All rights reserved.

Name ______________________________ Date ____________

Words with the VCCV Pattern

Basic: Write the Basic Word that best fits each clue.

1. get pleasure from
2. an error
3. a human being
4. where flowers grow
5. opposite of *remember*
6. a baseball official
7. a command
8. protects your head
9. opposite of *solution*
10. soft floor covering

1. ____________________ 6. ____________________

2. ____________________ 7. ____________________

3. ____________________ 8. ____________________

4. ____________________ 9. ____________________

5. ____________________ 10. ____________________

Spelling Words

Basic

1. person
2. helmet
3. until
4. carpet
5. Monday
6. enjoy
7. forget
8. problem
9. Sunday
10. garden
11. order
12. mistake
13. umpire
14. herself

Challenge

expect
wisdom

Challenge: Write two sentences about how you might help a friend reach a goal. Use both of the Challenge Words.

____

____

____

© Houghton Mifflin Harcourt Publishing Company. All rights reserved.

Name ______________________ Date ____________

The Foot Race Across America
Spelling: Words with VCCV Pattern

Word Sort

Write each Basic Word next to the correct heading.

Vowel *a* in first syllable	
Vowel e in first syllable	
Vowel *i* in first syllable	
Vowel *o* in first syllable	
Vowel *u* in first syllable	

Challenge: Add the Challenge Words to your Word Sort.

Spelling Words

Basic

1. person
2. helmet
3. until
4. carpet
5. Monday
6. enjoy
7. forget
8. problem
9. Sunday
10. garden
11. order
12. mistake
13. umpire
14. herself

Challenge

expect
wisdom

© Houghton Mifflin Harcourt Publishing Company. All rights reserved.

Name ____________________ Date ____________

The Foot Race Across America
Spelling: Words with VCCV Pattern

Proofreading for Spelling

Find the misspelled words and circle them. Write them correctly on the numbered lines below.

Spelling Words

Basic

1. person
2. helmet
3. until
4. carpet
5. Monday
6. enjoy
7. forget
8. problem
9. Sunday
10. garden
11. order
12. mistake
13. umpire
14. herself

Some Really Super Softball!

Last Sundy, the Braden Bobcats' fans got a big thrill when the Bobcats beat the Pinehill Pumas.

The game was tied 1–1 in the last inning. The Bobcat batters came up in ordor. First came Polly Peters, who looked ready to win that game all by herrself. The Puma pitcher, though, couldn't find the plate, and the umpeire called four balls in a row. Polly walked to first base.

The next persen up to bat was Miko Myata. This time, the Puma pitcher's probblem was wild pitches. When one pitch hit Miko's helmit, Miko strolled to first base and Polly moved to second.

The pitcher made one last misteak when he threw a perfect pitch. Shayla Smith swung mightily. CRACK! That ball was out of the park, and it probably didn't land untill Munday. The Bobcats won it, 4–1!

1. ____________ 6. ____________
2. ____________ 7. ____________
3. ____________ 8. ____________
4. ____________ 9. ____________
5. ____________ 10. ____________

© Houghton Mifflin Harcourt Publishing Company. All rights reserved.

Name ______________________ Date ____________

Abbreviations for Days and Months

The Foot Race Across America
Grammar
Abbreviations

- An **abbreviation** is a shortened form of a word. Most abbreviations begin with a capital letter and end with a period.

  Monday; Mon.

  August; Aug.

Thinking Question
Is the word a day of the week or a month of the year?

Write the correct abbreviation for each day and month.

1. Sunday ____________
2. December ____________
3. Tuesday ____________
4. Thursday ____________
5. Saturday ____________
6. November ____________
7. Wednesday ____________
8. September ____________
9. Friday ____________
10. February ____________

Copyright © Houghton Mifflin Company. All rights reserved.

Name ______________________ Date ____________

Abbreviations for Places

- An **abbreviation** is a shortened form of a word.
- Places with names that can be abbreviated include roads, streets, lanes, avenues, and boulevards. Examples include *Harrison Rd.*, *Maple St.*, *Elmira Ln.*, *Plainville Ave.*, and *Broad Blvd.*

Thinking Question
Is the word the name of a place?

Write each place name correctly. Use capital letters and abbreviations.

1. King Boulevard ______________________
2. Jefferson Street ______________________
3. Western Avenue ______________________
4. Oak Road ______________________
5. Chestnut Lane ______________________
6. Ocean Boulevard ______________________
7. Washington Street ______________________
8. Smith Lane ______________________
9. Vermont Avenue ______________________
10. Lincoln Street ______________________

© Houghton Mifflin Harcourt Publishing Company. All rights reserved.

Name ______________________ Date ____________

Writing Abbreviations

1–5. Write the correct abbreviation for each day and month.

1. Tuesday ____________

2. January ____________

3. Friday ____________

4. October ____________

5. Saturday ____________

6–10. Abbreviate each place name correctly.

6. Myer Lane ____________

7. Hudson Street ____________

8. Prospect Road ____________

9. Lynn Boulevard ____________

10. North Avenue ____________

© Houghton Mifflin Harcourt Publishing Company. All rights reserved.

Name ______________________ Date ____________

The Foot Race Across America
Grammar: Spiral Review

Possessive Nouns

- A **possessive noun** shows that a person, an animal, or a thing owns or has something.
- To show that **one** person, animal, or thing has possession, add an **apostrophe** and *-s* **(*'s*)**.
- To show that **more than one** person, animal, or thing has possession, add an *-s* and an **apostrophe** **(*s'*)**.

Noun	Singular Possessive Noun	Plural Possessive Noun
teacher	teacher's	teachers'
book	book's	books'

Activity: Write the word in parentheses as a possessive noun to complete the sentence.

1. __________ home is in Oklahoma. (Andy)

2. He runs in his ________ neighborhood. (cousin)

3. Andy likes to run with the ________ children. (neighbors)

4. He times his running with his ________ stopwatch. (sister)

5. The ________ prize is a huge trophy. (winner)

6. The ________ families all watched the race. (runners)

7. Allen could hear the _______ chirps as he ran. (bird)

8. Each __________ shirt had a number. (contestant)

9. Every runner could hear the _______ cheers. (fans)

10. The ________ statue of Andy shows him running. (town)

© Houghton Mifflin Harcourt Publishing Company. All rights reserved.

Name ____________________ Date ____________

Conventions: Proofreading

Proofreading your work for correctly spelled **abbreviations** will make your writing stronger.

Incorrect Abbreviation	Correct Abbreviation
tues; mar	Tues.; Mar.
av; rd	Ave.; Rd.

Use proofreading marks to write abbreviations correctly in this informal note.

Sun, Oct 3

Liam,

We stopped by Pleasant Str on fri and met your uncle's family. He is a wonderful man, and his kids and wife are great, too. We met Pat Smith, who is very nice. He lives in Miami. He has a house on Beach Blvd, near the ocean. We are going to meet him and Cindy Birch next Tues for a clambake.

Lucy

Proofreading Marks
¶ Indent
∧ Add
Delete
≡ Capital letter
/ Small letter

© Houghton Mifflin Harcourt Publishing Company. All rights reserved.

Name ______________________ Date ____________

Focus Trait: Organization

Read each sentence that gives a comparing or contrasting detail. Write whether it compares or contrasts.

______________ Andy Payne and Peter Gavuzzi both competed in the International Trans-Continental Foot Race.

______________ Both men were called "Bunioneers."

______________ Andy was from Oklahoma, while Peter was from England.

______________ Andy won in 1928, but Peter won in 1929.

Think of a topic sentence for a paragraph that compares Andy and Peter. Write the sentence. Then write a topic sentence for a paragraph that contrasts Andy and Peter.

Comparing paragraph:

____

____

Contrasting paragraph:

____

____

© Houghton Mifflin Harcourt Publishing Company. All rights reserved.

Name ____________________ Date __________

Double Consonants

Choose a syllable from the left box and a syllable from the right box to make a word that completes each sentence. Write the word on the line and read the completed sentence.

Hint: Each word you make will have a double consonant.

First Syllables					Second Syllables				
at	but	dol	fun	hap	den	der	lar	low	nel
lad	sud	tun	yel	zip	ny	pen	per	ter	tract

1. A magnet will ____________ a needle.
2. What do you think will ____________ next in that story?
3. Bonnie needs a ____________ marker to color the sun.
4. I spread ____________ on warm toast.
5. All of a ____________, it started to rain.
6. I can't close my jacket because the ____________ is broken.
7. Climb up the ____________ carefully.
8. That joke was so ____________ that I hurt myself laughing.
9. Jake has one ____________ to buy a treat.
10. A mole will dig a ____________ under the ground.

© Houghton Mifflin Harcourt Publishing Company. All rights reserved.

Name ______________________ Date ______

Reader's Guide

The Power of Magnets

Your Magnet Invention

Now is your chance to design a magnet to make your life easier! First, answer the questions below to make sure you understand how magnets work. Then, create your own design.

Read pages 20–21. What causes some objects to be attracted to a magnet?

____

____

Read page 22. What happens if you sprinkle iron filings around a magnet?

____

____

Read page 23. What is important about electromagnets?

____

____

Read pages 24–25. How can you create a magnetic field in your own home?

____

____

© Houghton Mifflin Harcourt Publishing Company. All rights reserved.

Name ______________________________ Date ______

The Power of Magnets
Independent Reading

Now think of a way that you can use a magnet to improve your life. Will you use the magnet in your home or outside? Will you use it at school? Will you use a regular magnet or an electromagnet? Draw a picture of your magnet and write an explanation of how it works. Be sure that you include details from the text in your design.

____

____

____

____

____

© Houghton Mifflin Harcourt Publishing Company. All rights reserved.

Name ______________________ Date ____________

Double Consonants

The Power of Magnets
Spelling: Words with Double Consonants

Basic: Write the Basic Word that best completes each group.

1. sheet, blanket, ______________
2. chapter, unit, ______________
3. dime, quarter, ______________
4. jam, preserves, ______________
5. fox, raccoon, ______________
6. top, side, ______________
7. postcard, note, ______________
8. peach, plum, ______________
9. milk, cheese, ______________
10. zipper, snap, ______________

Challenge: Use one of the Challenge Words to write a sentence.

____

____

____

Spelling Words

Basic

1. jelly
2. bottom
3. pillow
4. happen
5. butter
6. lesson
7. cherry
8. sudden
9. arrow
10. dollar
11. hello
12. rabbit
13. letter
14. button

Challenge

stubborn
mirror

© Houghton Mifflin Harcourt Publishing Company. All rights reserved.

Name ______________________ Date ____________

Word Sort

The Power of Magnets
Spelling: Words with Double Consonants

Write each Basic Word next to the correct heading.

Words with three letters in both syllables	____________	____________
	____________	____________
	____________	____________
	____________	____________
	____________	____________
	____________	____________
Words with two letters in one of the two syllables	____________	____________
	____________	____________
Words with four letters in both syllables	____________	____________

Spelling Words

Basic

1. jelly
2. bottom
3. pillow
4. happen
5. butter
6. lesson
7. cherry
8. sudden
9. arrow
10. dollar
11. hello
12. rabbit
13. letter
14. button

Challenge

stubborn
mirror

Challenge: Add the Challenge Words to your Word Sort.

© Houghton Mifflin Harcourt Publishing Company. All rights reserved.

Proofreading for Spelling

Find the misspelled words and circle them. Write them correctly on the lines below.

Dear Jamal,

Can you believe you're getting a leter from me, at last? I think of you a lot, especially when I see a jar of that charry jellie you love so much. Mom bought some the other day, and all of a suddin, I find that I love it, too!

One of my front teeth fell out last week. I put the tooth under my pilloaw. The next morning, a doller showed up there. Maybe that's enough to buy a treat for my pet rabit.

Hey, you're a science buff, right? Do you happan to know much about magnets? We had a really neat lessone on them in science class last week, and I'd love to talk to you about them.

Well, say hellow to your family for me. Please write back if you can. I miss you!

Your friend,

Curtis

Spelling Words

1. jelly
2. bottom
3. pillow
4. happen
5. butter
6. lesson
7. cherry
8. sudden
9. arrow
10. dollar
11. hello
12. rabbit
13. letter
14. button

1. ______________ **5.** ______________ **9.** ______________

2. ______________ **6.** ______________ **10.** ______________

3. ______________ **7.** ______________

4. ______________ **8.** ______________

© Houghton Mifflin Harcourt Publishing Company. All rights reserved.

Contractions with *not*

You can put together two words and make a **contraction.** An apostrophe (') takes the place of any letter or letters that are left out. Many contractions combine a verb with *not.* The contraction *won't* is special. You form it from the words *will not* and change the spelling.

It ***is not*** *always easy to invent something.*
It ***isn't*** *always easy to invent something.*
Michael Faraday ***was not*** *afraid to try something new.*
Michael Faraday ***wasn't*** *afraid to try something new.*

Thinking Questions
Which verb am I putting together with the word not? Which letter should I leave out and replace with an apostrophe?

Write the contraction for the words in parentheses. Use an apostrophe in place of the underlined letter or letters.

1. Electromagnets ______________ work unless they are turned on. (do n<u>o</u>t)
2. The magnet in the poem ______________ get used anymore. (does n<u>o</u>t)
3. A computer's hard drive ______________ work correctly without an electromagnet. (will n<u>o</u>t)
4. We ______________ aware that doorbells use electromagnets. (were n<u>o</u>t)
5. A blow dryer also ______________ work without an electromagnet. (would n<u>o</u>t)
6. The poem's speaker ______________ been allowed to make her brother disappear. (has n<u>o</u>t)
7. I ______________ see a magnetic field, but I know it exists. (can<u>no</u>t)
8. I ______________ believe all the things magnets do! (could n<u>o</u>t)

© Houghton Mifflin Harcourt Publishing Company. All rights reserved.

Name ________________________ Date ____________

Contractions with Pronouns

The Power of Magnets
Grammar:
Contractions

You can put a pronoun and a verb together to make a contraction. An apostrophe replaces the letter or letters that are left out.

*She says that **she is** working on a project.*
*She says that **she's** working on a project.*

***We will** see if it turns out.*
***We'll** see if it turns out.*

Thinking Question
When I join a pronoun with a verb, which letters should I leave out and replace with an apostrophe to make a contraction?

Write the contraction for the words in parentheses. Use an apostrophe in place of the underlined letter or letters.

1. ____________ be exciting to find out if the experiment works. (It <u>wi</u>ll)
2. ____________ read a lot about experiments with magnets. (We <u>ha</u>ve)
3. Make sure ____________ ready for the science fair. (you <u>a</u>re)
4. ____________ going to enter the science fair, too. (I <u>a</u>m)
5. ____________ judge whose project is the best. (They <u>wi</u>ll)
6. ____________ going to be competitive. (It <u>i</u>s)
7. ____________ almost finished our project. (We <u>ha</u>ve)
8. She says ____________ enter the science fair next year. (she <u>wi</u>ll)

© Houghton Mifflin Harcourt Publishing Company. All rights reserved.

Name ______________________ Date ____________

Contractions

1–5. Write the contraction for the words in parentheses. Use an apostrophe in place of the underlined letter or letters.

1. We ______________ gone to the science fair before. (have n<u>o</u>t)
2. My family ______________ know how much fun it would be. (did n<u>o</u>t)
3. My sister ______________ stop playing with the projects. (would n<u>o</u>t)
4. My brother ______________ wait to enter the science fair himself. (can<u>no</u>t)
5. We ______________ mind competing against each other. (will n<u>o</u>t)

6–10. Write the contraction for the words in parentheses. Use an apostrophe in place of the underlined letter or letters.

6. ______________ going to love the science fair. (You <u>a</u>re)
7. My teacher says ______________ won a prize. (I <u>ha</u>ve)
8. ______________ give it to me later. (She <u>wi</u>ll)
9. ______________ hang in my bedroom. (It <u>wi</u>ll)
10. ______________ the best prize I ever won. (It <u>i</u>s)

© Houghton Mifflin Harcourt Publishing Company. All rights reserved.

Name ______________________ Date ____________

Writing Proper Nouns

- A **proper noun** always begins with a capital letter.
- Days, months, holidays, historical periods, and special events are proper nouns.
- The first, last, and important words in a book title are capitalized. Book titles are underlined.

Proper Nouns	
day	Wednesday
month	March
holiday	Thanksgiving
book title	The Giver

Activity: Write all proper nouns and book titles from each sentence correctly.

1. The electricity went off last friday. ____________
2. I read my favorite book, the dark forest, with a flashlight.
   ____
3. We saved a lot of electricity in april. ____________
4. My book report on Michael Faraday is due after memorial day. ______________________
5. I would rather learn about world war II than about electricity. ______________________
6. My sister is writing a book called when the lights go out.
   ____

© Houghton Mifflin Harcourt Publishing Company. All rights reserved.

Name ______________________ Date ____________

Conventions: Proofreading

Sentences Without Correct Contractions	Sentences with Correct Contractions
Shes making her project.	She's making her project.
The project is'nt too difficult.	The project isn't too difficult.
We have't decided what we'll make.	We haven't decided what we'll make.

Proofread the paragraphs. Find and underline five mistakes in the spelling of contractions. Write the correct sentences on the lines below.

Theyr'e starting to organize this year's science fair. I cann't miss it this time! Last year I was'nt able to get a project done in time. This year I'm going to make sure I do.

Iv'e heard the fairs are a lot of fun. You get to see all the projects other people have worked on. I would'nt want to miss that.

1. ______________________________
2. ______________________________
3. ______________________________
4. ______________________________
5. ______________________________

© Houghton Mifflin Harcourt Publishing Company. All rights reserved.

Focus Trait: Ideas

Read each problem and solution. Add details to elaborate. Explain how the problem was solved and how the solution works. Use information from "The Power of Magnets."

1. **Problem:** Kaylie dropped a box of pins.
Solution: She used a magnet.

Details:

____

____

2. **Problem:** The remote control car does not work.
Solution: We put a battery in it.

Details:

____

____

3. **Problem:** A junkyard owner needs to move a car.
Solution: He flips a switch.

Details:

____

____

4. **Problem:** Michael Faraday wanted to produce electricity.
Solution: He moved a magnet through a coil of wire.

Details:

____

____

© Houghton Mifflin Harcourt Publishing Company. All rights reserved.

Name ______________________ Date ____________

Words with *ough*, *augh*

Read each word in the box. Say the sound that *ough* or *augh* stands for. Then write the word in the chart under the correct category.

Word Bank					
bought	caught	fought	naughty	rough	taught
brought	daughter	laugh	ought	sought	thought

ough* rhymes with *paw	***ough* rhymes with *puff***	***augh* rhymes with *paw***	***augh* rhymes with *staff***

© Houghton Mifflin Harcourt Publishing Company. All rights reserved.

Name ______________________ Date ______

Reader's Guide

Becoming Anything He Wants to Be

Create a Captioned Illustration

This story of Erik Weihenmayer is told with photographs that have captions. The photographs help us see what Erik can do, and the captions help us understand the photographs. Let's take a closer look.

Look at page 35. What does the caption let you know about the photograph on this page?

____

____

Look at page 37. What does the caption tell you about the photograph on this page?

____

____

Look at page 38. In the first photograph, which of the bike riders is Erik? How do you know?

____

____

The caption for the second paragraph tells us why this story is important for everybody. Why is it important?

____

____

© Houghton Mifflin Harcourt Publishing Company. All rights reserved.

Name ______________________ Date ________

Becoming Anything He Wants to Be
Independent Reading

Erik Weihenmayer achieved amazing things. How have his achievements inspired you? What is one thing you would like to do but think you cannot do? Draw an illustration of yourself doing this difficult thing. Write a caption that explains what you are doing.

____

____

____

____

© Houghton Mifflin Harcourt Publishing Company. All rights reserved.

Name ______________________ Date __________

Becoming Anything He Wants to Be
Spelling: Words with *ough* and *augh*

Words with *ough* and *augh*

Basic: Write the Basic Word that completes each sentence.

1. A mother and her ______________ had a problem.
2. The little girl had ______________ a bad cold.
3. Every day, the child's ______________ grew worse.
4. Her sore throat made her voice ______________ and scratchy.
5. The girl couldn't sleep ______________ the night.
6. The mother knew she ______________ to take the girl to a doctor.
7. They didn't have ______________ money, though, to pay the bill.
8. Then the mother ______________ of something.
9. Some of her neighbors had ______________ to have a free clinic set up nearby.
10. She picked up her daughter and ______________ her to the clinic.

Challenge: Write a sentence about a problem you had and how you solved it. Use both Challenge Words.

____

____

____

Spelling Words

Basic

1. taught
2. thought
3. rough
4. laugh
5. bought
6. cough
7. ought
8. caught
9. fought
10. daughter
11. tough
12. through
13. enough
14. brought

Challenge

sought
naughty

© Houghton Mifflin Harcourt Publishing Company. All rights reserved.

Name ______________________ Date ____________

Becoming Anything He Wants to Be
Spelling: Words with *ough* and *augh*

Word Sort

Write each Basic Word beside the correct heading.

Words in which the letters *gh* are not pronounced	
Words in which the letters *gh* are pronounced /f/	

Spelling Words

Basic

1. taught
2. thought
3. rough
4. laugh
5. bought
6. cough
7. ought
8. caught
9. fought
10. daughter
11. tough
12. through
13. enough
14. brought

Challenge

sought
naughty

Challenge: Add the Challenge Words to your Word Sort.

© Houghton Mifflin Harcourt Publishing Company. All rights reserved.

Name ______________________ Date ____________

Proofreading for Spelling

Find the misspelled words and circle them. Write them correctly on the lines below.

Not long ago, our old dog, Bella, stopped coming when we called her. At first, we thouht she just wanted to show us who was boss. After all the training she'd had, though, she aught to know better.

Then the vet found Bella's problem: she had lost her hearing. We worried that Bella would have a tuff time in a silent world. That sweet girl has tawght us a thing or two!

First, we baught a book about living with a deaf dog. We read throogh it carefully. We learned to talk to Bella with body signals, not our voices. In a few days, using an arm to beckon her brout her to us right away. When it was time for a walk, we held up a leash for her to see. That was ennough to get her racing to the door!

Today, we luagh to think we ever worried about Bella. She fougt to overcome her problem, and she's an even more amazing dog now.

Spelling Words

1. taught
2. thought
3. rough
4. laugh
5. bought
6. cough
7. ought
8. caught
9. fought
10. daughter
11. tough
12. through
13. enough
14. brought

1. ____________
2. ____________
3. ____________
4. ____________
5. ____________
6. ____________
7. ____________
8. ____________
9. ____________
10. ____________

© Houghton Mifflin Harcourt Publishing Company. All rights reserved.

Name ______________________ Date __________

Commas in a Series

- A **series** is a list of three or more words together in a sentence.
- Use a **comma** to separate the words in a series.

  It was cold, wet, and windy when he climbed the mountain.

Thinking Question
Is there a list of three or more words in the sentence?

Activity: Rewrite each sentence correctly. Add commas where they are needed.

1. He had a big breakfast of eggs toast and orange juice.

____

____

2. She packed up the tent backpack and sleeping bag.

____

____

3. The weather was cold windy and sunny.

____

____

4. They wore sunglasses hats and gloves.

____

____

5. Along the path they saw deer raccoons and a fox.

____

____

6. They would tell their story to Anna Julio and Wade.

____

____

© Houghton Mifflin Harcourt Publishing Company. All rights reserved.

Name ______________________ Date ____________

Commas with Introductory Words

- Use a **comma** after the introductory words *well*, *yes*, and *no*.
- Use a comma after order words such as *first*, *second*, *next*, and *finally*.
- Do not use a comma after *then*.

Yes, I might want to try climbing one day.

Thinking Question
Is there an introductory or order word in the sentence?

Rewrite these sentences correctly. Add commas where they are needed.

1. First let's have some lunch.

____

2. Yes that is a very good idea.

____

3. No I did not remember to fill the water bottles.

____

4. Well we will have to look for a water fountain.

____

5. Yes I can show you how to pack away the blanket.

____

6. First fold it neatly in half and then in half again.

____

7. Next smooth out any wrinkles.

____

8. Finally roll the blanket carefully, starting at one of the short ends.

____

© Houghton Mifflin Harcourt Publishing Company. All rights reserved.

Name ______________________ Date ____________

Commas in Sentences

Read each pair of sentences. Fill in the circle next to the sentence that uses correct punctuation.

1. Ⓐ Climbers can be tall, short, young, or old.
Ⓑ Climbers can be tall short, young or, old.

2. Ⓐ Yes, climbing is one of my hobbies.
Ⓑ Yes climbing is one of my hobbies.

3. Ⓐ Well reaching, a goal takes lots of hard work.
Ⓑ Well, reaching a goal takes lots of hard work.

4. Ⓐ She used paper, markers, and scissors to draw her plan.
Ⓑ She used paper, markers, and scissors, to draw her plan.

5. Ⓐ First, you have to decide if you are willing to do the work.
Ⓑ First you have to decide if you are willing to do the work.

© Houghton Mifflin Harcourt Publishing Company. All rights reserved.

Name ______________________ Date ____________

Writing Abbreviations

- An **abbreviation** is a short way to write a word. Most abbreviations begin with a capital letter and end with a period.

Abbreviations	
Sunday	Sun.
Monday	Mon.
September	Sept.
title for any woman	Ms.
title for married woman	Mrs.
street	St.
avenue	Ave.

1–10 Write each abbreviation correctly.

1. October ______________________
2. avenue ______________________
3. Tuesday ______________________
4. doctor Smith ______________________
5. Thursday ______________________
6. mister Hill ______________________
7. December ______________________
8. April ______________________
9. mister Adams ______________________
10. street ______________________

© Houghton Mifflin Harcourt Publishing Company. All rights reserved.

Name ______________________ Date ____________

Sentence Fluency:
Combining Words to Form a Series

Choppy Sentences	Combined Nouns to Make a Series
He needs rope for climbing. He also needs gloves for climbing. He needs boots for climbing.	He needs rope, gloves, and boots for climbing.

Choppy Sentences	Combined Predicates to Make a Series
He wrestles. He scuba dives. He rides a bike.	He wrestles, scuba dives, and rides a bike.

Activity: Combine each group of sentences by forming a series of nouns, verbs, or phrases. Write the new sentence on the lines. Add commas where necessary.

1. Erik climbs walls. He climbs mountains. He also climbs hills.

____

____

2. Jose wants to share his success with his parents. He wants to share it with his friends. He wants to share his success with his neighbors.

____

____

3. Anika never gave up. She never complained. She never made excuses.

____

____

4. Fong practiced in the morning. He practiced at night. He practiced on the weekend. ______________________________

____

© Houghton Mifflin Harcourt Publishing Company. All rights reserved.

Name ______________________ Date ____________

Focus Trait: Word Choice

Read each step of the instructions for starting a rock collection. Rewrite the step with exact words and details to give more information.

1. **Step:** Get a box.

   With Exact Words and Details:

   ____

2. **Step:** Dig up some rocks.

   With Exact Words and Details:

   ____

   ____

3. **Step:** Clean the rocks.

   With Exact Words and Details:

   ____

   ____

4. **Step:** Put them away.

   With Exact Words and Details:

   ____

5. **Step:** Read about the rocks.

   With Exact Words and Details:

   ____

   ____

© Houghton Mifflin Harcourt Publishing Company. All rights reserved.

Name ______________________ Date ____________

Words Ending in *-er* or *-le*

Read the words in the box. Then choose the word that best matches each clue.

Word Bank				
apple	better	farmer	little	member
middle	rattle	struggle	summer	supper

1. a red fruit that is sweet to eat	____________
2. someone who belongs to a group	____________
3. a meal you eat late in the day	____________
4. not big; small	____________
5. a person who grows food crops	____________
6. a toy that a baby shakes	____________
7. in between the first and the last	____________
8. the opposite of *worse*	____________
9. the opposite of *winter*	____________
10. a fight or something difficult	____________

© Houghton Mifflin Harcourt Publishing Company. All rights reserved.

Reader's Guide

A New Team of Heroes

The Story of the Game

Choose a character to tell about the soccer game in his or her own words. First, review the play to remember important details.

Read pages 48–50. What can we tell about Carla so far?

____

____

What do we learn about Lauren?

____

____

How does Hiro feel about Carla?

____

____

How does Gayle feel about Carla?

____

____

Read pages 51–52. What can we tell about Manny?

____

____

© Houghton Mifflin Harcourt Publishing Company. All rights reserved.

Name ______________________ Date ______

Think about the characters in the play: Carla, Lauren, Hiro, Gayle, and Manny. Imagine that one of the soccer players is writing a narrative about the game from his or her point of view. Use the box below to write the story.

My Story by ______________________

____

____

____

____

____

____

____

____

____

____

© Houghton Mifflin Harcourt Publishing Company. All rights reserved.

Name ____________________ Date __________

Words Ending with *-er* or *-le*

Basic: Write the Basic Word that answers each clue.

1. The goal of someone who is making funny faces at you is to make you do this. ____________
2. If your aunt is married, her husband is this. ____________
3. Your goal is to make this color when you mix red and blue. ____________
4. An archer's goal is to hit this part of a target. ____________
5. A goal you plan to reach tomorrow is one you'll reach at this time. ____________
6. Eating one of these a day can help you reach your goal of keeping the doctor away. ____________
7. If a rooftop is your goal, this tool can help you. ____________
8. Cooking a turkey dinner is the goal of many people in this month. ____________
9. People often have a goal of building a snowman during this season. ____________
10. A common goal during this season is to stay cool. ____________

Spelling Words

Basic

1. apple
2. river
3. little
4. October
5. ladder
6. summer
7. purple
8. later
9. November
10. giggle
11. uncle
12. winter
13. center
14. double

Challenge

whistle
character

Challenge: Write two sentences telling how someone might reach a goal. Use both Challenge Words.

____

____

© Houghton Mifflin Harcourt Publishing Company. All rights reserved.

Name ______________________ Date ____________

Word Sort

A New Team of Heroes
Spelling: Words Ending with *-er* or *-le*

Write each Basic Word next to the correct heading.

Words that name seasons	
Words that name months of the year	
Words that name objects you can pick up	
Other words	

Spelling Words

Basic

1. apple
2. river
3. little
4. October
5. ladder
6. summer
7. purple
8. later
9. November
10. giggle
11. uncle
12. winter
13. center
14. double

Challenge

whistle
character

Challenge: Add the Challenge Words to your Word Sort.

© Houghton Mifflin Harcourt Publishing Company. All rights reserved.

Proofreading for Spelling

A New Team of Heroes
Spelling: Words Ending with *-er* or *-le*

Find the misspelled words and circle them. Write them correctly on the lines below.

Try Out for the Basketball Team

Welcome back to school! We hope your sumer vacation was super.

As you all know, winnter is the season for basketball. This year, tryouts for our team will be held the last Monday in Ocktober. Practices will begin early in Novembar. In January, we'll travel across the rivier to play our first game against the Dunkers.

We urge all interested students, new or old, big or littel, to try out for the basketball team. You won't have to make a basket from the senter of the court. You must, though, be willing to dubble your efforts when it's needed.

So if you'd like to see yourself in our team's purpul uniform, just try out. That way, you won't be sorry laiter that you didn't.

Spelling Words

1. apple
2. river
3. little
4. October
5. ladder
6. summer
7. purple
8. later
9. November
10. giggle
11. uncle
12. winter
13. center
14. double

1. ____________ 5. ____________ 8. ____________

2. ____________ 6. ____________ 9. ____________

3. ____________ 7. ____________ 10. ____________

4. ____________

© Houghton Mifflin Harcourt Publishing Company. All rights reserved.

Name ____________________ Date __________

What Is a Preposition?

Common Prepositions

about	around	beside	for	near	outside	under
above	at	by	from	of	over	until
across	before	down	in	off	past	up
after	behind	during	inside	on	through	with
along	below	except	into	out	to	without

Underline the preposition in each sentence.

1. Some people like to hike the trails around a lake.
2. Hiking over the hills is good exercise.
3. In summer, flowers cover the hills.
4. Some people like the mountains in winter.
5. They ski or snowboard down the steep slopes.
6. A high mountain is a challenge for climbers.
7. Reaching the top of a mountain is a climber's goal.
8. Climbers usually hike with a guide.
9. Guides know the safest way to the top.
10. Which mountains in our country do you know about?

© Houghton Mifflin Harcourt Publishing Company. All rights reserved.

Name ______________________________ Date ____________

Prepositional Phrases

A New Team of Heroes
Grammar:
What Is a Preposition?

1–5. Underline the prepositional phrase in each sentence.

1. Those people in the distance are taking a hike.
2. I wonder how far they will hike before lunch?
3. We can follow the hikers up the hill.
4. My friend from the city likes hiking, too.
5. Let's hike to that tall pine tree.

6–10. Underline two prepositional phrases in each sentence. Write the prepositional phrase that tells *when*.

6. On Friday, our class took a hike in the woods.

   ____

7. I didn't think we were going on the hike until next week.

   ____

8. We rested beside a creek at noon.

   ____

9. During our rest, we looked at a distant mountain.

   ____

10. By the afternoon, we were all very tired from the long hike.

   ____

© Houghton Mifflin Harcourt Publishing Company. All rights reserved.

Name ______________________ Date ____________

A New Team of Heroes
Grammar:
What Is a Preposition?

Prepositional Phrases

1–5. Underline the prepositional phrase in each sentence.

1. We use mountains for many things.
2. Rock climbers like to climb up mountain cliffs.
3. Miners search the rock for metals.
4. Trees growing on mountains supply logs for houses.
5. Cows and sheep can graze around a mountain's base.

6–10. Underline the prepositional phrases in each sentence. Write the prepositional phrase that tells *where*.

6. The weather on a mountain can change in a few minutes.

   ____

7. It is very cold at the top of a mountain.

   ____

8. At great heights, there is little oxygen for breathing.

   ____

9. Many of the world's highest mountains are in Asia.

   ____

10. Very few people live on these high mountains.

    ____

© Houghton Mifflin Harcourt Publishing Company. All rights reserved.

Name ______________________ Date __________

Kinds of Adverbs

- An **adverb** is a word that describes a verb.
- **Adverbs** can come before or after the verb they are describing.
- Adverbs tell *how, when,* and *where* an action happens.

Adverb That Tells How	Adverb That Tells When	Adverb That Tells Where
Manny **quickly** passed the ball.	We have to practice **often.**	We practice **here** at the park.

1–4. Write the adverb and what it tells about each underlined verb.

1. Gayle cheered loudly for Manny. ______________
2. They ran away from the fire. ______________
3. The game always begins at 4:00. ______________
4. Our team shook hands happily with the other team.

____

5–8. Rewrite the sentences below into one sentence.

5. The team played another game. They played the game later.

____

6. The goalie blocked the ball. He did it easily.

____

7. We stop for water breaks. We stop often.

____

8. Manny scores a goal. He always scores a goal.

____

© Houghton Mifflin Harcourt Publishing Company. All rights reserved.

Name ______________________ Date ____________

Sentence Fluency

Short, choppy sentences can be combined to make your writing smoother. You can combine two sentences by **moving a prepositional phrase**.

Two Sentences	Combined Sentence
We watched the film about mountains. We watched the film on Tuesday.	We watched the film about mountains on Tuesday.

Combine two short choppy sentences by moving a prepositional phrase to combine two sentences. Write the new sentence on the line.

1. The map is on the wall.
   The map is behind Mrs. Brown's desk.

   ____

2. We can see the mountains in Asia.
   We can see the mountains on the map.

   ____

3. Please show me the mountains of Africa.
   Please show me the mountains on the map.

   ____

4. We will learn more about mountains.
   We will learn more after lunch.

   ____

5. Have you ever hiked in the mountains?
   Have you ever hiked in our state?

   ____

© Houghton Mifflin Harcourt Publishing Company. All rights reserved.

Name ______________________ Date ____________

Focus Trait: Ideas

Read each pair of sentences. Underline the fact. Draw a line through the opinion. Then write a fact to replace the opinion.

1. In football, a touchdown scores 6 points. It is easy to score points.

Fact: ____

2. Golf is the hardest sport. Golfers use clubs to hit the ball.

Fact: ____

3. Swimmers should wear red suits. Many swimmers begin at a young age.

Fact: ____

4. A baseball catcher wears a mask. Everyone should have a turn to catch.

Fact: ____

5. All schools should have sports teams. Many children play sports.

Fact: ____

© Houghton Mifflin Harcourt Publishing Company. All rights reserved.

Name ______________________ Date ____________

Sort the Words

Saving Buster
Phonics: Schwa Sound

Read each word in the box. Find the vowel that makes the schwa sound. Then write the word in the chart under the spelling of the schwa sound.

Word Bank					
about	actor	alive	cactus	camel	circus
engine	kennel	pencil	pilot	salad	wagon

schwa spelled *a*	schwa spelled *e*	schwa spelled *i*

schwa spelled *o*	schwa spelled *u*

© Houghton Mifflin Harcourt Publishing Company. All rights reserved.

Name ______________________ Date ______

Reader's Guide

Saving Buster

Pet Reporter

You are a reporter. You are going to write a newspaper article about Buster's accident and how the neighbors helped. Newspaper reporters ask questions to find facts for their stories. Use the questions below to find facts. Then write the newspaper article.

Read pages 66–67. What happened to Buster?

____

____

Read page 68. What is the problem that Donovan wants to help solve?

____

____

Read pages 70–71. What was Donovan's idea for solving the problem?

____

____

Read pages 72–73. Did Donovan's solution raise the $2,000 needed to pay for Buster's care?

____

____

© Houghton Mifflin Harcourt Publishing Company. All rights reserved.

Name ______________________ Date ______

Now you know the facts about Buster's accident and how the neighborhood helped solve the problem. It is time to write your article for the local paper. Remember to include a headline or title for your story and an illustration.

NEWS

© Houghton Mifflin Harcourt Publishing Company. All rights reserved.

Name ______________________ Date ____________

Words that Begin with *a* or *be*

Saving Buster
Spelling: Words that Begin with *a* or *be*

Basic: Write the Basic Word that completes each sentence.

Spelling Words

Basic
1. below
2. about
3. belong
4. around
5. again
6. alone
7. because
8. above
9. between
10. alive
11. behind
12. begin
13. along
14. before

Challenge
awhile
beyond

1. I was walking ____________ my street when I spotted a kitten.

2. When it ran ____________ my legs, I fell over!

3. Dad guessed the kitten is ____________ two months old.

4. Dad said I could bring the kitten inside ____________ it was cold out.

5. Then the kitten hid in a dark place ____________ the couch.

6. ____________ I could get it out, I had to move furniture.

7. The kitten jumped up on a shelf ____________ the fireplace.

8. It followed a toy ____________ in a circle.

9. The kitten made me laugh over and over ____________ .

10. Dad and I agree that the kitten and I ____________ together.

Challenge 11–12: Write two sentences about animals. Use both Challenge Words.

____

____

© Houghton Mifflin Harcourt Publishing Company. All rights reserved.

Name ______________________ Date ____________

Saving Buster
Spelling: Words that begin with *a* or *be*

Word Sort

Write each Basic Word next to the correct heading.

Second syllable has three letters	
Second syllable has four letters	
Second syllable has five letters	

Challenge: Add the Challenge Words to your Word Sort.

Spelling Words

Basic

1. below
2. about
3. belong
4. around
5. again
6. alone
7. because
8. above
9. between
10. alive
11. behind
12. begin
13. along
14. before

Challenge

awhile
beyond

© Houghton Mifflin Harcourt Publishing Company. All rights reserved.

Name ______________________ Date ____________

Proofreading for Spelling

Saving Buster
Spelling: Words that Begin with *a* or *be*

Find the misspelled words and circle them. Write them correctly on the lines below.

Monday, July 9

This past weekend, our family took part in a barn raising. I'd never heard abowt these events befoar. In a barn raising, a lot of people who bilong to a community get together to build a barn. No community member has to face the huge job of building a barn aloan.

At first, I just walked arround the barnyard. I didn't know where to bigin to help. Soon, a man called from a beam abuve me. "Son, could you please bring me some nails?" he asked. I leaped into action becauze I wanted to be part of the group. I set up a ladder balow the man and handed him the nails.

After that I worked hard all weekend, and that barn is done. It's a beauty! I would sure love to be part of a barn raising agenn.

Spelling Words

1. below
2. about
3. belong
4. around
5. again
6. alone
7. because
8. above
9. between
10. alive
11. behind
12. begin
13. along
14. before

1. ____________
2. ____________
3. ____________
4. ____________
5. ____________
6. ____________
7. ____________
8. ____________
9. ____________
10. ____________

© Houghton Mifflin Harcourt Publishing Company. All rights reserved.

Name ____________________ Date __________

Using *I* and *Me*

Saving Buster
Grammar: Correct Pronouns

- Use the pronoun *I* only as the subject of a sentence. Always capitalize the word *I*.

  I am going to school.

- Use the pronoun *me* only as an object pronoun. When you talk about another person and yourself, it is polite to list yourself last.

  Julie handed the books to Lucy and **me**.

Thinking Question
Is the pronoun the subject or the object of the sentence?

Activity: Write the pronoun *I* or *me* to complete each sentence.

1. __________ watched my dog chase the ball.
2. Dad and __________ entered a dish in the potluck contest.
3. Amy went to the vet with my dog Sparky and __________.
4. My service dog helps __________ cross the street.
5. Can __________ help you plan the contest?
6. __________ liked the pasta salad the best.
7. The judge couldn't decide, so she gave the first prize to both Andy and __________.
8. __________ own a black dog named Ruby.
9. Ruby has been with my sister and __________ since I was five years old.
10. Someday __________ would like to train puppies to be service dogs.

© Houghton Mifflin Harcourt Publishing Company. All rights reserved.

Name ______________________ Date ____________

Pronouns and Homophones

Saving Buster
Grammar: Correct Pronouns

Homophones are words that sound alike but have different spellings and different meanings. Be sure to choose the correct homophone. Using the wrong homophone changes the meaning of the sentence.

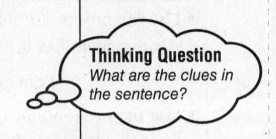

Thinking Question
What are the clues in the sentence?

Homophone	Meaning	Example
its	belonging to it	The dog wagged **its** tail.
it's	it is	**It's** very cold outside.
your	belonging to you	I like **your** watch.
you're	you are	**You're** going to be late!
there	at or in that place	The book is over **there**.
their	belonging to them	**Their** dog can do tricks.
they're	they are	**They're** going to the store.

Activity: Read the sentences. Circle the correct homophones.

1. Dog training can be a fun activity for both you and **your** **you're** dog.
2. **Its** **It's** important to work with your dog every day.
3. Dogs perform best when **their** **they're** praised for good behavior.
4. If **your** **you're** patient with your dog, you can teach him or her to roll over.
5. **It's** **Its** important to train a puppy.
6. You can buy a leash at a pet supply store. Ask a clerk to help you when you get **there** **they're.**
7. The best time to train **your** **you're** dog is when he or she is young.
8. Dogs can still be trained when **there** **they're** older, too.

© Houghton Mifflin Harcourt Publishing Company. All rights reserved.

Name ____________________ Date ____________

Saving Buster
Grammar: Correct Pronouns

Correct Pronouns

Read each pair of sentences. Fill in the circle next to the sentence that uses the correct pronoun.

1. Ⓐ Mom and I will make dinner.
   Ⓑ Mom and me will make dinner.

2. Ⓐ The dog brought the ball to Marisa and I.
   Ⓑ The dog brought the ball to Marisa and me.

3. Ⓐ They're dog was trained to be a service dog.
   Ⓑ Their dog was trained to be a service dog.

4. Ⓐ It's fun to teach a dog to do tricks.
   Ⓑ Its fun to teach a dog to do tricks.

5. Ⓐ I saw your mom at the store.
   Ⓑ I saw you're mom at the store.

© Houghton Mifflin Harcourt Publishing Company. All rights reserved.

Name ______________________ Date ____________

Making Comparisons

- **Adjectives** describe nouns. They can also show how people, places, and things are alike and different.

Comparing with Adjectives		
compare two	add *-er*	taller
compare three or more	add *-est*	tallest

- **Adverbs** describe verbs. For adverbs that end in *-ly*, add ***more*** to compare two actions. Add ***most*** to compare three or more actions.

1–4. Write the correct form of the adjective in parentheses to complete each sentence.

1. Molly was the ______________ of all the service dogs. (small)
2. The Smiths were ______________ than our other neighbors were. (friendly)
3. Of all of her classmates, Liz's voice is the ____________. (strong)
4. Doug was the ____________ member of the class. (young)

5–6. Rewrite the sentences, combining each pair of sentences.

5. Ralph is smarter than the cat. He is quicker too. ______________

____

6. Of all the dogs in the park, Benny has the biggest feet. He also has the longest tail. ______________________

____

© Houghton Mifflin Harcourt Publishing Company. All rights reserved.

Name ______________________ Date ____________

Conventions

Sentence with incorrect use of *I* and *me*	Corrected sentence
Me and my mom did everything we could to help out.	My mom and I did everything we could to help out.

Sentence with incorrect homophone	Corrected sentence
Their cooking wonderful food for the dinner tonight.	They're cooking wonderful food for the dinner tonight.

Proofread each sentence. Check for the correct use of the pronouns *I* and *me* and the correct use of homophones. Write the corrected sentence on the line.

1. David and me think the cooking contest will be fun.

____

2. They gave they're food to me and my mom.

____

3. The dog left the bone over their.

____

4. Its amazing how much money was raised.

____

5. Me and my friends think it's important to help you're neighbors.

____

6. Its good when people help each other.

____

7. You can help them by watching there dog.

____

8. They're dog loves to play.

____

© Houghton Mifflin Harcourt Publishing Company. All rights reserved.

Name ____________________ Date __________

Focus Trait: Organization

Read each paragraph. Cross out the detail that does not tell about the main idea. Then add a fact or a detail sentence that supports the main idea.

1. Other animals pull vehicles. Oxen pulled pioneers' wagons in the 1800s. Locomotive trains can pull many cars. Some kinds of horses pull sleighs and carriages.

____

____

2. Several types of animals carry people. For hundreds of years, people have ridden horses. Donkeys can carry people through rough terrain. Lots of kids ride bicycles to school. Some people also ride camels.

____

____

3. In a beehive, different bees have different jobs. The queen lays eggs. Worker bees do a few jobs. They help make wax. They also feed other bees and help protect the hive. Some people are allergic to bees.

____

____

4. Dogs do different kinds of work. Chihuahuas are a tiny kind of dog. There are herding dogs and police dogs. Some dogs are even actors!

____

____

© Houghton Mifflin Harcourt Publishing Company. All rights reserved.